Turning Points

Defining Moments that Shaped the Character of Top Business Leaders

Randy Schuster

Turning Points

Published by Indaba Press

Indaba, Inc.

Treasure Island, FL 33706-1105

727-360-0111

www.Indaba1.com

www.21Laws.com

ISBN – 13: 978-1-58570-209-1

Printed in the United States of America.

Table of Contents

Foreword

You can do anything you want in life as long as you have the heart and the passion to do it.

If there's anything you should take away from this book, it's that single truth. All that stands between you and success is your desire, what you think about, and the belief to achieve your dreams.

If you want proof of that, then the book you're presently holding can offer it in spades.

As you read the stories in this book, you're going to come to a realization: success can come from virtually anywhere. These are the stories of dozens of highly successful individuals who come from a variety of backgrounds and circumstances, no two of which are alike. Each of them will share with us what they consider to be their "turning points"; experiences that have both influenced and helped to put them firmly on the path to success.

It's my hope that the more you learn about the people, places and times that influenced the successful entrepreneurs in this book, the more you'll come away with the feeling that your own story could easily fit into these pages right next to them.

You will read stories ranging from individuals who started out with a goal no more lofty than saving money for a car, to those who made staggering vows to own their own business by age thirty; from individuals who lived through turbulent decades and faced all types of discrimination, to those who had to overcome internal obstacles in the form of disabilities; from individuals who grew up in a family business that they helped drive to new heights of success, to those who started literally from nothing. The odds are good that you'll recognize yourself in a lot of these people.

This book is written in such a way that you should be able to just pick it up and read a story or two whenever you happen to have a spare moment. My advice is not to read it all at once. Rather, keep it on hand and carry it around with you, so that you can consult it at your own leisure. My hope is that in so doing, you'll have something to constantly inspire you - to remind you that **it's not where you've come from that matters, but where you're going**. And where you're going is something that is entirely up to you.

I sincerely hope that reading this book will become a turning point in helping you realize your dreams. Enjoy reading.

- Randy Schuster

Dedication

This book is humbly dedicated to many people. All of them have been extremely important in shaping the direction of my life, and I don't know what I would do without them.

To my wife Erni Schuster, who is a real partner in the truest sense of the word. As we've grown together over the years, she has given me the freedom and support I needed in order to realize all my dreams. None of this would be possible without her.

To my children Danny and Matt Schuster. Some of the best turning points in my life have come about from being a father and watching them grow and learn. I'm eternally grateful for all the lessons that they've taught me and look forward to many more. Danny, your no limit personality never fails to make me smile. Matt, you've never heard the word "no" in your life. Your incredible perseverance and tenacity is an inspiration.

To my father Marty. I've learned so much from him through the years. For all the things that enabled me to have my own turning points when I realized I wanted to become an entrepreneur, and all that has happened since, I credit you.

To my mother Jacquie, who is the heart and soul of the family. None of us could have made it where we are today without you to hold us together.

To Delia Costanzo, who pulls it all together, even when it seems impossible. To Marie Eizenarms, for coordinating and planning; your efforts are indispensable. To Sharon Rollins, who is the master at juggling more than anyone ever thought possible. To Kris Dussmann, for the many roles that you play. To Jim Cerone, for all your support and guidance. To Hellen Davis, for your coaching and mentorship. To Howie Jacobson, for his creativity, vision and support. To Julie-Ann Amos and Rick Woodson, for all your assistance with editing this work.

And last but not least, let me take a moment to extend my most sincere gratitude to the wonderful people who took the time to contribute to this book, as well as those who referred me to them. Understand that this book would never have happened without you.

Introduction: Danny Wegman

"The only mistake you can make in life is to not set your sights high enough."
- Robert Wegman

When Randy first approached me and asked me to write this foreword, I have to admit that I was somewhat at a loss as to what to talk about. He told me that the whole purpose of the book was to highlight a number of successful individuals and to examine what points in their lives were most influential in shaping them to become the successes that they are.

When I spoke with Randy about this, he didn't seem to be nearly as concerned as I was. The two of us simply began to talk with one another about the nature of Wegmans Grocery Stores - the business that my family and I run. Randy seemed more interested in the stores than just about anyone I've ever met. The way he spoke about how "big" our stores are in the industry, and how out-of-towners come to

Rochester just to visit a Wegmans, really began to open my eyes about how things looked from the outside.

In no time at all, he had me talking about my past and the origins of our company. When Wegmans first started up, it went through the same tough times that are bound to plague any start up business. My grandfather and great uncle owned it jointly, but after the death of my grandfather, my great uncle exercised his right to buy out the whole business. At that point, my own father was really removed from the picture as far as ownership goes, although he stuck at it, working in our family business full time except for his stint in World War II. In fact, shortly after he returned from the war in 1947 my uncle died and my father was able to purchase the Wegmans business back from my great uncle's estate. It's remained with our immediate family ever since.

The family business in many ways is all that I've ever known. It might be because of this, that it was hard for me to think of myself as an individual who had a real "turning point" - some instant when a bolt out of the blue came and turned everything around for me. However, talking with Randy, I began to realize just how much the atmosphere I had grown up in had really defined me.

When I was growing up, we lived on a farm. The nearest kids my age were some two and a half miles away, so as you might imagine with two older sisters I spent virtually all of my time with them (my third sister had not yet been born). If there was something I wanted to do, it was pretty much a necessity for me to be able to sell the idea to them. Of course, there were plenty of times that they got me interested in their own activities as well, just because there was no one else around.

It might not sound like much, but these experiences did quite a lot to help shape my current worldview. If you ask me, **it's not possible to succeed in today's world on your own**. It's a world that absolutely demands collaborative efforts, and more than anything, I attribute this mindset with much of the success that Wegmans has enjoyed over the years.

It went beyond just my sisters, of course. As I said we lived on a farm, so there was quite a lot of communal spirit. We could count on the assistance of other nearby farms, who knew that in turn they could count on us. We were always lending equipment back and forth, or just doing little things here and there to help one another out. To me, that's the real spirit of business – and even today, some of my good friends are my biggest competitors.

While talking with Randy helped turn me on to the notion that even very little things could add up to a defining element in somebody's life, there was one other thing that occurred to me that I'd like to share with you.

> *In 1967 my father was visiting Thailand and was scheduled to give a speech that would touch upon his insights in the world of business. As it turns out, the person who was scheduled to speak before him took so long that my father never actually got to give his speech! However, he had written it down in preparation, so I was able to get a copy of it. I can't tell you how much of an effect that little speech had on me.*

> *It was essentially my father's entire knowledge of business encapsulated into a few short pages. He spoke passionately about the importance of creating your own niche in life and doing something that is totally unique; something that only you can do. He also emphasized that whatever you do, there will come a time when you have to be able to adapt it to the changing times, because if one thing is certain, it's that the times are always changing.*

I took away from that letter the philosophy, when coupled with my feelings on the importance of collaboration, that this basically sums up the way I try to do business today:

> **"The purpose of being in business is to give people a choice that they wouldn't have had otherwise – and to do it in a way that the competition can't easily emulate."**

As our interview came to an end, I was surprised at just how much my background has really influenced the way my life has gone. I realized that there's really no event, no person, no moment too small or insignificant that it can't be the single most important thing to somebody. There is no such thing as a life without a turning point, whether that moment spans years and years or it happens in the blink of an eye.

I'd like to challenge the readers of this book to examine their own lives and to look for what they consider to be their own turning points. Perhaps, like me, you'll look at the stories in this book and think that these are people who are in a different class entirely - that your own story is nowhere nearly as interesting as theirs. Let me assure you, if you look at your life with the right perspective, this is not the case. When I stopped to think about my turning points, it helped me to think more clearly about the way I help to run the family business, and how I should go about doing it in the future. It was about a lot more than just patting myself on the back for past successes; it was about learning more about myself and getting ready for ever greater future successes. I feel confident that everyone reading this book can do the same thing for themselves.

All the best,

Danny Wegman

<u>Matt Augustine</u>

CEO of Eltrex Industries

"No one can make you feel inferior without your consent."
Eleanor Roosevelt

Matt Augustine's path to success has been marked by more obstacles than many of us will ever have to deal with. However, this very hardship instilled in Matt from a very young age the desire to not only succeed himself, but to change the way things work, so as to facilitate the success of others as well. From his days as a student, Matt has consistently found himself in need of summoning up his courage in order to face obstacles head-on without flinching. The combination of this resilience and the desire to create a better life for himself and others has given Matt the edge that he needed to become truly successful.

It all started primarily because of the place and time that Matt was born into. He was born in Georgia, but soon thereafter moved to another southern state, Louisiana, just before the civil rights movement would start hitting its major

1

strides. This wasn't an ideal environment for African American families such as his. From a very young age, Matt's parents helped to prepare him for the hardships that they knew he was bound to face, by telling him that if he wanted to succeed at the same level as others, he would need to work at least twice as hard in order to overcome the discrimination that would naturally be leveled against him because of his race. This proved to be quite true. Matt had to work very hard throughout school, but nevertheless he did succeed in earning grades high enough to enter the University of Southwestern Louisiana.

College campuses at that time were not places noted for their acceptance of people from all stripes of life. Rather, they had long been a homogenized world that was just recently seeing the influx of liberalism that would lead to the "turbulent times" that Matt recalls having to contend with on a daily basis. So intense was the persecution Matt faced that he had to engage in bitter fights with the University staff for more than a year, just to be granted the right to live on campus.

This kind of treatment didn't sit well with Matt, so he decided that he would **be the kind of person who actively works to bring about changes within the system**. He soon found himself getting involved with campus societies and clubs that were dedicated to the ideals of social reform. Given that he attended school in the mid 1960s, this was a time period that saw more than its fair share of protests and demonstrations. Matt's efforts with these groups were a valuable learning experience for him.

Matt's experience at the University of Southwestern Louisiana came to a head when one of his professors attempted to sabotage his academic career. Despite Matt's having the highest grade in his class, the professor in question gave him an F for the course on the grounds that he had missed too many days of class. Despite the fact that Matt had not actually missed any days, he was at a loss as to how to prove his innocence, due to the fact that attendance wasn't officially kept. He continued to be a victim of the system he had been working to change.

Tired of contending with the politics of academia, Matt left school to join the Marine Corps, where he served in Vietnam and did exceptionally well for himself. Working within military intelligence, Matt was awarded many honors and a top level security clearance. It was only after this success that his turning point came.

When he returned home, Matt continued to struggle with discrimination as a result of political unrest and the escalating civil rights movement. He was fortunate enough to meet with two professors who knew of his academic and service records, and they suggested that Matt apply to the Harvard Business School where they had both received doctorate degrees.

Matt enrolled and quickly found himself an active part of life on campus. He once again was appointed leader of many student organizations and societies that were dedicated to fighting discrimination. He particularly recalls steps that he took to bring global awareness to the somewhat insular and conservative Harvard campus by protesting the tragic events that had happened at Kent State and Morgan State. Despite managing all of those obligations, Matt still found the time to run his own successful business with friends on the side, putting in an average of 60 to 80 hours a week. In addition, he carried some of the highest grades in his class.

While Matt was doing well at Harvard, Joe Wilson, the founder of Xerox Corporation, helped start a manufacturing company that would be dedicated to giving African

Americans job opportunities. Despite their noble aims, however, the management was simply not up to the task of running the business aptly named Fighton Inc., and so they embarked on a nationwide search for an entrepreneur who could turn the organization around. They found Matt.

The activist nature of the business appealed to him, and he was quickly brought on in order to turn things around. As he puts it: **"We beat the odds, but it wasn't easy."**

This quote personifies the approach that Matt has taken with all of his ventures, both personal and professional, over the years. A dedication to rooting out the causes of failure and injustice and working to change them has given him a degree of success that has been matched by few.

Because of his adherence to these principles, Matt indeed succeeded in turning Fighton Inc. around. Without sacrificing the principles of the organization, Matt changed their public persona by adopting the name of Eltrex Industries, and diversifying the company's manufacturing base to cover just about every aspect of the industry that presented a niche.

Recently, Matt was named as one of Rochester's 50 most successful businessmen over 50, being inducted into the Business Hall of Fame in 2002. Going on the momentum of his success at Eltrex Industries, Matt continues to **find ways to give back to the community and work towards social change.** He's intimately involved with efforts to raise money for black scholarships to give inner city youth the opportunity to receive the same kind of education that he had. In addition, he served as a Distinguished Minuett Professor at the Rochester Institute of Technology, where he worked to impart his unique blend of business sense and social consciousness to a new generation of entrepreneurs. Today, he's looking to expand his skills even further by pursuing his doctorate in Executive Leadership. This pursuit was made possible thanks to the efforts of an individual who received her own doctorate in part because of one of Matt's scholarships. This is a testament to the sweeping changes that Matt has created in his life.

Though he still faces discrimination from time to time, Matt looks on today's business environment as a place where there are a lot more opportunities for African Americans and repressed people of all stripes. Though he is modest about his own involvement, there's no doubt that at least some of the credit for this change goes to his own efforts, and his tireless dedication to change for the better.

Turning Points

<u>Ted Boucher</u>

President and CEO of Caldwell Manufacturing Company

"To serve, to strive, and not to yield."
Outward Bound Motto

Ted Boucher describes his turning point as one that serendipitously followed him throughout the course of his life, subtly influencing all of his passions along the way - although he didn't realize it until many years later. When he eventually became aware of what that influence really meant, he would go on to use it to turn his family's business into one of the most successful in both the industry and in the region. Ted didn't start out with that goal in mind because at the start he had no intention of ever working for the family business. How he went from one extreme to the other is the story of that subtle, defining influence.

When he was in high school, Ted and the other students were treated to something of an advantage. At that point in time, 1969, computers were just beginning to take off. Many businesses were seeing the advantage of using them, but most couldn't afford their own. As a result, those who owned computers, such as universities, could sell off blocks of time to companies who wanted to use those computers but still didn't have the extensive need for their own system to justify the huge expenditure of owning one. Ted's high school was one of the first in the country to use this principle in the school itself. They brought in a computer system and made it freely available to all the students. Not only could the students take advantage of the word processing capabilities, but they were also required to learn simple programming in order to graduate.

When Ted went on to Dartmouth College, where he majored in geology, this influence followed him. Dartmouth was also one of the first colleges in the nation to feature computer terminals that were freely accessible to all the students. He became intimately familiar with programming and all the different ways that a computer could streamline the process of data collection and interpretation, making it much easier to all who were involved. Though his passion still lay almost solely in geology, in particular marine geology, this influence by computers would end up taking Ted to places he hadn't anticipated.

Fresh out of school with his Masters degree, Ted went to work for Gulf Oil. He worked with them by looking for oil off the north shore of Alaska and had quite a leg up on the rest of the employees working in that area. Whereas they were trained only in more outdated modes of geological exploration, Ted was able to use his extensive knowledge of computers to quickly move ahead in the company. After working there only six months he got his first lesson in just how much of a lead his computer expertise gave him: his supervisor came to him and told him he was being sent off to Anchorage to negotiate for the purchase of data critical to the Alaskan oil drilling industry. He was told, "try not to spend more than five million dollars," which was incredibly shocking to someone newly out of graduate school who had been subsisting largely on beans and rice!

Ted recalls being very nervous and overwhelmed at the prospect of handling so much responsibility. He called around as much as he could, seeking advice from as many in his company as he possibly could, until he felt he knew enough to advance. His negotiations were eventually successful, and he came in under budget, a fact that he attributes largely to the way he handled that stressful and demanding situation.

After two years of working for Gulf, an old high school girlfriend named Peggy came back into Ted's life, and their relationship began to get somewhat serious. She and Ted took a look at where his prospects with Gulf were going to lead him; he didn't seem to have a lot of opportunity anywhere except in small towns that didn't appeal to either him or Peggy. As such, he decided to go back to business school and get his MBA.

Back in business school, the influence of computers continued to follow Ted. He worked with them extensively and even had the opportunity to work with cutting edge programs such as Lotus 123, thanks in large part to taking classes with the niece of Lotus founder, Mitch Kapor. The decision to return to business school proved to be a very timely one for Ted. He married Peggy, and then after graduating saw that the oil industry was in the middle of a record slump. Prices were bottoming out and no one was hiring anywhere. Ted took a look back at his life and began to see the influences that had followed him throughout high school. As he puts it, **"I did what I should have done all along."**

Ted went to work for a computer company, Data General, and was involved in many high profile assignments including working on the industry's first laptop computer, the Data General One. Though he was given a lot of responsibility and seemed to be in a very promising position, something happened that would change everything.

The business owned by Ted's family, Caldwell Manufacturing, had long been a successful supplier to window manufacturers throughout the country. Ted's father had been approached by venture capitalists who sought to buy him out, and as a result, he called a family meeting to discuss the option to sell.

Despite his intention to never work with the family business, Ted took a look at the numbers, ran them through a model that he constructed on his computer, and quickly realized that there were a lot of opportunities to take this company even further without selling out, if only certain areas could be shored up and made more efficient. Moreover, he felt that while he would always be a small player in big companies like Gulf and Data General, he could do big things as a leader at Caldwell. Ted's father agreed to give Ted the chance, but he had to apply for a position just like anyone else.

Ted applied to come to work for his family's business, and despite a rocky start, he was soon introducing computers into the company in a way that streamlined every aspect of the business.

When Ted arrived, the company had two largely unused word processors, which were functioning more as paperweights. Under Ted's influence, the company purchased a single personal computer that was shared by 12 offices. Eventually, computers began to be used in the engineering department for computer assisted drafting, by secretaries for their word processing needs, and indeed all throughout the company.

Ted was able to prove the worth of these advancements when the sales department offered a projection to the president that if they could reduce their turnaround time on sales from 17 to 5 days, they could double their market share. Though the president was skeptical that it could be done, Ted knew that it could. Using computers to transfer a serial process into a largely parallel one that made everyone's work proceed simultaneously, he was able to reduce the company's turnaround time to 5 days in just under a year. What was then an incredible achievement is now an industry standard.

After the success of their new "5 day standard", the company began to reinvent the company's brand image, insisting on an all new logo and packaging to replace that which the company was presently using; material that had been in use, unchanged, for over 100 years. The end result is that Caldwell is now one of the most recognizable names in the industry, and Ted is now CEO of the company.

Although he never envisioned himself in this position when he first started out, he can look back and see the path that was laid out for him, making it almost inevitable that he would arrive here. However, it wouldn't have happened without his ability to apply an industrial revolution like computers to those areas that he felt passionate about, carving out a niche for himself that he could carry over into any industry successfully.

Turning Points

<u>Arunas Chesonis</u>

Chairman and CEO of PAETEC

"Leadership is more doing than dash."
Peter Drucker

Arunas Chesonis had his turning point a little later than most, but if the success he was to go on to achieve is any indication, he didn't suffer from the delay.

The real story of Arunas started when he was in college. Faced with the task of working in teams on sometimes seemingly impossible assignments, Arunas found that the success or failure of his ideas hinged primarily upon the people that he could convince to become involved with him, plus of course, if he was willing to put in the requisite hard work. It was a lesson gradually learned, and it wouldn't become fully cemented in his consciousness, it wouldn't become real to him, until a situation that he would face later in his career.

After college, Arunas went on to work with a telecommunications company known as ACC at a job that he found much to his liking. The managers were always open and straightforward with the employees, and Arunas had the freedom to speak openly with his co-workers and form the bonds necessary to achieve true, functional teamwork. However, these comparatively idyllic days weren't to last long.

In 1997, Arunas came to hear that mega-conglomerate Teleport/AT&T was planning to buy out ACC and take over operations. At first, he was excited about what such a prospect might mean, but he became severely disillusioned with how things were handled in reality. He would approach the incoming managers to question them about what policies they would be changing, who they intended to keep on, and all manner of questions that were essential to his continuing to perform his job well. However, unlike his managers at ACC, Arunas found that the Teleport/AT&T managers weren't anywhere near as open with him. They refused to share information that Arunas considered critical, preferring to keep the books closed for no valid reason that he could see.

Furthermore, Arunas realized that the incoming managers were not sharing all the integration plans with his fellow employees. Arunas and the rest of the employees were shocked to find that Teleport/AT&T had not thought about the long term value of retaining ACC veterans. The final straw came when Arunas and his fellow officers at ACC found out that Teleport/AT&T was not interested in retaining their employment contracts. Arunas had had enough. He thought back to his days in college when he realized that successful teamwork was contingent entirely upon the people involved, much more so than the principles.

"You can think of an idea... but to make it happen, you have to really believe it, work hard at it and get the right people involved."

He realized that the people from Teleport/AT&T who had taken over ACC didn't share similar corporate philosophy. Furthermore, he realized that the good people that he was working with, the ones who were about to go their separate ways, were exactly the type who could easily get things done when called upon to do so. It was a once in a lifetime opportunity and Arunas was prepared to seize upon it. He decided to leave the company. He resolved to start his own telecommunications company and to create a company that shared the same values and beliefs that had helped make him successful.

He went over the company roster and handpicked the 75 people he felt would be the best to work with in his new company, PAETEC Communications. Wanting to make a dramatic impression, he wrote all of their names on a whiteboard in red, and when he would call these people to speak with them about joining up with him, he would show them this whiteboard. If they agreed to part ways with Teleport/AT&T and risk joining his new enterprise, he would erase their name and rewrite it in green. Arunas had originally thought he might get ten or eleven recruits at most and that this would be an ideal core to build a new business from. However, he underestimated the level of company-wide dissatisfaction. By the time he had finished negotiations, he had secured the services of 71 of the 75 people on his dream team list.

Thus prepared, Arunas and his group drafted a new business plan over the summer, directly tailored to compete against what they saw as the worst of the policies of others in the telecommunications industry. To put the matter simply, the main focus of the plan was simply to **"do the right thing" and treat people with respect as individuals**. After that, the plan was to raise money. Much like Arunas had anticipated, his group worked together with almost perfect synergy, and the plan they drafted was enough for them to quickly secure all the money necessary to get their company underway.

Of course, their rise was not without a small setback. Seeing the potential success of their competing plan, Teleport/AT&T tried to sue PAETEC to stop them from moving forward. The lawsuit only succeeded in bringing more publicity and attention to PAETEC, and people hungry for a different approach to the telecommunications game quickly signed on with them. After only 15 months, Arunas's dream team company had raised 46 million dollars in equity, a success that nobody could ignore.

To this day, PAETEC remains an incredible success. Still, when asked how he feels about it, Arunas is quick to tell anyone that success isn't a matter of business to him. Rather, it's a matter of how he's reached his success: namely, by focusing on people and always doing the right thing. Without this outlook, he says he wouldn't have any of the loyal employees and customers that he now enjoys, and without them, he would be nowhere. It is this focus on ethics and the power of individuals that formed the basis of his turning point, and that has also gone on to help him achieve the great success that he now enjoys.

<u>Kathy Clark</u>

CEO of Clark Moving and Storage, Inc.

*"For every failure, there is an alternative course of action;
you just have to find it. When you come to a road block,
take a detour."*
Mary Kay Ash

Kathy Clark's turning point is one that many people can share and sympathize with.

In March of 1998, at the age of 42, she was diagnosed with breast cancer. Although a diagnosis as serious as cancer always tends to bring about big changes, it was the changes that her sickness forced upon her professional life that were the most significant to Kathy. Until that point, Kathy had been trying to live out two extremes: a business owner overseeing her company, and someone who actually performed the job duties of every role in the company. After

17

being forced to step back and let others assume some of the responsibility during her treatment, she has found a new level of enjoyment and satisfaction with her work.

In order to understand exactly how Kathy got to this point, though, we have to look back at her origins and upbringing. She was born into a family that owned its own business, a company based in Syracuse, NY called Material Handling Products. She was the youngest of three siblings with two older brothers. Though it had always just been naturally assumed that one of her brothers would be the one to take over the family business, this did not lessen Kathy's aspirations any. She set a goal from a very young age, a dream of owning her own business before she was thirty.

Certainly, Kathy's home life was one that supported this kind of ambition. Growing up with two older brothers, she naturally felt a sense of competition and the desire to try and emulate them. Her parents supported this, telling her that anything the two boys did, she could also do if that was her desire. As a result, she never felt inhibited or restrained at all because of her gender. In fact, it was during a particularly adventurous outing involving skydiving that she met Rich Clark, who would one day become her husband!

When Kathy went on to college, she would experience what at the time appeared to be something of a temporary setback. Because of her zestful approach to life she became preoccupied with too much partying and flunked out in her sophomore year. Not eager to face her parents, who were none too pleased at this turn of events, she went to live with a friend in Rochester. How she came to this decision is fairly interesting. From a young age, she had always felt a somewhat mysterious calling to the area. She recalls being enchanted by the yellow Kodak boxes that would arrive at her home carrying slides ordered by her father, an amateur photographer. The city of Rochester always held a mystique for her that she never quite understood, so she jumped at the chance to move there when the opportunity presented itself.

Looking for work, Kathy placed an application with a temp agency, who quickly found her work with the Mayflower agency, a moving company. Though at first her only job was to file papers and perform other clerical style work, her attitude eventually caught the attention of management who decided to give her a shot in the sales department. As it turns out, Kathy took to this quite naturally. She says that rather than feeling inhibited because of being a woman, it actually made it easier for her to get ahead. The uncommon sight of a woman in door to door sales allowed her to get her foot in the door a lot easier and seemed to command attention. In her own words:

> **"You have to find something that gives you the advantage, and when you find it, take advantage of it until it goes away."**

Take advantage she did. Within just a short amount of time, Kathy was one of the top salespeople in the company and had a huge list of customer accounts that she did constant business with. It was with shock then, that she came to her workplace one day in 1985 to find that the front gates were padlocked and the place was deserted. It had shut down literally overnight. Not wanting to disappoint the customer base that she had worked so hard to build up, Kathy went immediately to a phone booth and began making calls to her competitors to find someone who could fill the needs of her customers, so that they wouldn't be left out in the cold. Her next move was to call those customers directly, explain what had happened, and make sure they were taken care of.

Kathy spoke with Mayflower who gave her permission to open a temporary office in the area, with the agreement that they would send people from the corporate office within a week to interview managers from local competitors, to see who would be best suited to take over the new office. When they were not able to find anyone, Kathy suggested that she might be the right person for the job. Although she wasn't taken seriously until she enlisted the help of her husband, who had a background in electrical engineering and flight instruction, she eventually became the franchisee of Mayflower and achieved the dream of owning her own business before she was 30 years old.

That was when the real work began for her. She would go into work at 4AM to get things in order for the rest of the day. When the crew began to arrive at 7AM, they would work and place calls until around 5PM, at which point she would don work clothes and help the others paint and wire up the office, to make it more presentable to customers.

It cannot be said that Kathy is a stranger to hard work. In fact, it was during this time that she first began to realize **that there's such a thing as too much work**. She recalls that like many young entrepreneurs, she was afraid to say "no" to clients, even if she thought she couldn't handle the job they were offering. One day, she ended up losing a very large client because of this, and learned the valuable lesson that one can't do everything by oneself.

This lesson really sank in after her diagnosis with cancer.

As Kathy was lying on the operating table waiting to go under, she realized that she was preoccupied with the thought of phone calls she'd have to make the next day and suddenly came to the realization that she needed to take a few steps back.

Recalling how her insistence on doing it all had once inhibited her company when they lost that big client, she saw that she was inhibiting the growth of the company now by not allowing her workers the autonomy and freedom to make mistakes.

Nowadays, Kathy has matured into the true picture of a business owner. She takes joy in watching her workers grow and develop, as she is able to guide them and trust them to get the job done, rather than try to be a one-woman corporation in and of herself. It wasn't until this turning point that Kathy really began to see her position for what it was, and was finally able to truly enjoy the success that she had earned.

Turning Points

David Cornell

CEO of Cornell Jewelers

"A man is literally what he thinks...You are today where your thoughts have brought you. You will be tomorrow where your thoughts take you."
James Allen

Despite the fact that the jewelry industry is one of the most competitive markets in the world, David Cornell has it in the palm of his hand. To what does he owe that success?

In the summer of 1972, David was confronted with something that for many was the ultimate sign of freedom, a high number of 265 in the Vietnam draft lottery; a number that gave him an automatic deferral. Suddenly free to drop out of school and do literally anything he wanted, David found he had no idea what he wanted to do. It was the complex process of introspection that he undertook to answer this question that would go on to mark his entire professional life, although he didn't know it at the time.

At the time, all that was on David's mind was a road trip inspired by the romantic notions he had received from reading John Steinbeck's *Travels with Charley*. David set out in his 1970 Chevy Nova with an assortment of camping gear and $500, intent on finding himself in what he referred to as "searching for David". He spent six months traveling and visiting with friends through 41 of the 50 states.

> *Finally, David ran out of money in Boulder, Colorado. There, he hooked up with a friend and worked construction jobs in order to save up money. This was to have a large impact upon him, teaching him the value of being passionate about what it is that one does, so that one isn't simply filling the role of a "job". Filled with renewed purpose, David took his savings and set out to the Sierras and then California for a time, before heading east again. He eventually ran out of money once again, this time in New Orleans, where he began to feel the thrill of his wanderlust beginning to dwindle. He contacted his father, who wired him a $500 loan in order to return home. Feeling as if he had purged his restlessness and reached a new understanding of himself, David returned home to find that he had now shed his previous anti-establishment persona and that the appeal of steady, fulfilling work had begun to grip him.*

With this new purpose in mind, David returned to school at Monroe Community College where for the first time in his life, he made the Dean's list. David approached his father, who was 66 and owned a very successful wholesale jewelry business in downtown Rochester with three other partners. Seeing that his father would soon be looking into retirement, David decided it was time to make some career decisions. At the advice of his father he decided to try out the jewelry industry for one year, since he already had a foot in the door.

That foot in the door didn't propel him straight into a CEO's office, of course. David started out in his father's company as the low man on the totem pole, but rather than balking at this, he returned to the introspective nature that led him on his defining journey and realized he should view it as something of a learning experience. David worked with one of the other partners in the business, Norman Lempert, and as he put it, "kept his mouth shut" while learning the jewelry business.

Although David was grateful for what he was learning from Norman, he did feel that his talents weren't truly being challenged. It wasn't until a buying trip with his father at the age of 22 that David truly fell in love with the industry. The two of them created a special bond as they visited vendors together. David recalls being amazed at his father's expertise at guessing what the prices for certain merchandise might be, at nothing more than a glance. Impressed by the respect that this niche talent gained his father, David soon realized that **the key to working out his own foothold in the company was to play off his own talents in a way that the others weren't capable of**. David set up a system of categorization known as "plot cards", which were 5 x 7 inch index cards that recorded essential information about particular jewels in the company's collection, such as the color grades of diamonds or various imperfections in a stone.

At last feeling himself a valued contributor to the company, David continued to approach his work with a renewed enthusiasm, and his relationship with Norman continued to grow stronger. In 1982, the partners within the company had begun to argue with one another and they began to sell off its most valuable inventory. The bickering went on for 2 years and finally, with no end in sight, Norman suggested that David buy out the remaining assets, believing that he had developed the talents to run things. David did so, and David Cornell & Company, Inc. was founded. To this day he remembers the first sale made in his own business; a pair of diamond earrings.

For most of the 1980 and 1990s, David and six employees operated a successful business with low overhead in downtown Rochester. This was a magic formula for success in the jewelry industry at that time, but it wasn't long before his introspective tendencies began to catch up to David again, and he found himself initiating a massive change to his business model in anticipation of industry-wide changes on the horizon. He closed his successful downtown operation and opened a new retail store on Monroe Avenue with 22 employees and a new focus on retail skills. Of course, these tactics were to be much emulated by competitors and brought David great success.

When asked to sum up the philosophy that makes him a success, David says:

"Change is difficult for many people, and I learned to recognize that change is inevitable. If you're not willing to embrace change, you'll fall by the wayside."

He points to his friend and mentor Glen Rothman for support. Glen and David started in the jewelry business at about the same time, and David remembers Glen saying, **"The more you learn, the more you earn."** Far from being a simple rejoinder to value one's education, David interprets this as a reminder to continually evaluate one's self and change, to always be growing. The motto hasn't just brought him success, as he's quick to point out. Glen was among the first to introduce branding to the diamond industry, marketing the wildly successful "Hearts on Fire" line of jewelry through David's store.

David shows no signs of changing his successful formula of introspection and self-growth. Recently, he was inspired by a speech he heard given by Walt Sutton, the author of the book *Leap of Strength*. He decided to take a personal retreat on his own in Skaneateles, NY, where he locked himself away from all distractions in a hotel room and pondered over where he had been in the first half of his life, and where he wanted to go in the second half. This led him to his current project: further building up his business, using his artistry and creativity to take things to an all new level where they've never been before.

David is an individual always on the lookout for fresh ideas. His commitment to introspection, self-evaluation and acceptance of change as a positive force in the market has allowed him to build his business into something truly unique and successful.

Turning Points

<u>José Coronas</u>

General Partner of the Trillium Group

"The shrimp that goes to sleep gets washed out by the current."
Cuban proverb

The story of José Coronas' success is one absolutely filled with turning points. From his early days in Cuba, to arriving in Miami as a Cuban refugee, and then on to Rochester, NY to work for Eastman Kodak Company and other ventures, José has come from humble beginnings to establish himself. He attributes his success to the variety of turning points that gave him the tools he needed to take advantage of the many opportunities that would arise in his life.

The first turning point in José's life was when he was 12 years old. His father was so adamant about the fact that José needed a high quality education that he sent the young boy to Havana, which was on the complete opposite side of the country. José found attending the school a very enlightening

experience. Unlike many high schools, José recalls that his school was focused above all else on bringing out the leadership in every student who attended. In fact years later when he was working in the United States, he recalls that when on business, he would occasionally run into graduates from his high school class!

Right after high school, José wondered what exactly he would do with himself, but his ability to choose was quickly eliminated by the takeover of Cuba by Fidel Castro. A believer in capitalism, José's father decided that he and the family should move to Miami for the time being, assuming that Castro's reign would last little more than a year or so. After the Bay of Pigs situation played out, it became clear to José and his family that they wouldn't be returning to Cuba anytime soon, and they applied for permanent resident status.

José worked in hotels for a while before deciding that he should take advantage of his time here by pursuing an advanced education. On one lunch break, he and a friend went to the University of Miami and innocently asked an admissions officer:

"What can I be in the next four years that will make the most money?"

This was the next turning point in José's life. On the admission officer's advice he enrolled in the University of Miami, studying to become an industrial engineer. The entire time he was in school, he continued to work to support himself with jobs at local hotels. Despite this extra effort, he was still able to graduate with honors.

During his junior year in college, José was told that certain companies in the US were hiring college students for summer jobs. He applied to quite a few, including Eastman Kodak in Rochester. It turned out that the application he sent in to

Kodak was reviewed by a man named Dick Fitts, who saw potential in him and decided to give him a chance. José traveled to Rochester and worked for them the summer of his junior year. They were so impressed by his performance that they invited him back after graduation to fill a permanent position, an offer that he readily accepted.

Working for Eastman Kodak over the years provided José with a lot of opportunities to improve and grow, and thanks to his upbringing he was able to take advantage of many of these opportunities. Kodak offered him the chance to enroll in the University of Rochester's Executive Development program to get his MBA, which would round out his technical engineering background. He earned his degree there while continuing to work for Kodak and received the Hugh Whitney award for excellence by earning the highest grades in the program.

Given renewed confidence by this sudden influx of business knowledge, José decided to challenge himself by stepping away from his position as an engineer and getting into the marketing aspect of the company; he served in various marketing positions in the US and Europe, rising to the position of vice president and general manager of the Bioproducts Division, a new biotechnology initiative for Kodak.

José would face a serious setback when he realized that Kodak was being forced to downsize due to challenges in the film industry. He knew that since biotechnology wasn't Kodak's main focus, his division was one that would likely get the axe. José knew he could easily transfer to another division of Kodak, but he liked what he was doing and wanted to continue it. So he set out to create a future for this division independent of Kodak, and met up with several other people that he knew who were involved in the field. The meeting took place in Lapland, Finland, 200 miles north of the Arctic Circle. Here they developed a plan to establish a joint venture between three companies: Cultor Limited, Genentech, and Kodak – combining to form Genencor

International. José became the first CEO of this joint venture and met with great success at it. Today, Genencor is a leader in the biotechnology field.

He continued to accrue business experience as a CEO, just as he had when he'd worked in marketing and in engineering. When the opportunity arose to take himself even further, José knew that he was ready for it. Kodak asked him to return and run the Clinical Diagnostics Division that he had worked in some ten years earlier. Using the skills he had gained from all the opportunities he had taken advantage of over the years, José was able to grow that division into a 500 million dollar business in just five years.

Just when José was growing a major Kodak division, the winds of Kodak changed again and the company decided to divest itself of its health business. This posed a new challenge for José, who led the sale of the division to Johnson and Johnson for $1 billion, a very successful outcome. After 2 years of running the business, José left the corporate world.

Today, José continues his successful trend by working as a partner at Trillium Group, a venture capital enterprise started up by two of his colleagues from Kodak. Together, they work to fund startup companies in the area, thereby completing the circle of opportunity and advancement that took him so far. Trillium is the leading private equity firm in Upstate New York.

If anything can be said about José's rise to success, it's that he learned very early on to take advantage of the leadership qualities within himself. Because of that, he was able to make the most out of every opportunity that came his way, even those that seemed as if they would be a setback, such as Kodak's downsizing.

The ability to turn a string of potentially bad situations into an endless chain of upwardly mobile success stories is the real sign of an entrepreneur, and José is a shining example of that. As José likes to say, **"be willing to go after something new, and don't be afraid of change."**

Turning Points

Holly Creek

In charge of HollyCreekHomes

"Far better is it to dare mighty things, to win glorious triumphs even though checkered by failure...than to rank with those poor spirits who neither enjoy much nor suffer much, because they live in a gray twilight that knows not victory nor defeat."
Theodore Roosevelt

Holly Creek's turning point came about in a way that might sound familiar to many people, thanks to similar experiences in their own teenage years. It's likely, however, that for them the situation didn't play out exactly like it did for Holly.

At the age of twelve, her father made a comment to her that, "if you work hard enough to earn your own money and you want to buy a car, then you pay for half and I'll pay for half." This led Holly to visualize that she wanted a pink mustang convertible. By age 16, taking a job at her family's business, she began to save money and made a minor adjustment to her ambition: the pink convertible became a new red Corvette with a T Top. What didn't change was her commitment.

Three years later, at the age of nineteen, Holly approached her father and announced that she was ready. "Ready for what?" he inquired, having totally forgotten about the comments he had made seven years earlier. Holly reminded him of his promise, and revealed the staggering sum that she had secretly been saving all that time, much more than most people would ever expect a nineteen-year-old girl to be able to save. Nevertheless, her father was true to his word, and that brand-new 1971 red Corvette marked Holly's first realization of the power of perseverance; setting goals and sticking to them over the long term.

Married at age 19 to her high school sweetheart, and having her first daughter at age 20, the worker bee instincts that Holly inherited from her father would not allow her to be satisfied with being a stay-at-home mother for very long. While walking at Pittsford Plaza one day with her daughter, Holly walked into Snow Country Ski Shop and applied for a part-time job. It didn't take long for owners Joan and Dick Osur to see Holly's potential, and they took her under their wing and introduced her to the business world, where she learned how to manage and run a business. For quite a long time, Holly never gave much thought to being an entrepreneur, preferring instead to work at Snow Country while caring for her young child. After the birth of her second daughter, Holly opted to be a stay-at-home mother for her two children while her husband Paul worked at a rather successful corporate job that easily supported them.

Everything changed, however, when Holly was 35 and her children reached the ages of four and eleven. Paul began to grow dissatisfied with the corporate life he was leading, despite the financial success it had afforded him. After much discussion with Holly, he eventually abandoned his lucrative position in favor of starting his own business. As with many businesses, Holly's husband's venture didn't take off right away, so the family was at a loss for how to continue supporting themselves. With her husband focusing on his new business, Holly decided to go back into the work force herself.

Holly started her job search at the top, by contacting one of the most successful real estate agencies in Rochester, New York, Judy Columbus Realty. Judy was finally won over after a total of seven interviews, and she hired Holly as her newest realtor. It was in her work as a realtor that Holly's flair for setting goals and sticking to them became her greatest asset. Because she knew exactly how much money her family would need to survive while her husband was building his business, Holly had a concrete idea of just how many sales she would need to make, and when she would need to make them. She set goals for herself on the number of houses that she sold and began to consistently meet those goals each and every month. Observing this, Judy Columbus took an additional interest in Holly and began to coach her, bolstering her confidence and coaxing her into setting consecutively higher goals.

What began as a method to start her business, tracking numbers and intense goal setting became a model to continue to take her business to even higher levels. This created an enormous amount of belief in setting and achieving goals. No matter how high Judy set the bar, Holly continued to meet her goals, and before long she was the most successful realtor in the entire office.

Holly continued to meet with success in the industry, earning various awards and consistently producing the most sales in her district, until one day she received a very rare honor: a position in the top ten producers in the entire country by the standards of ERA Real Estate, a national real estate brokerage firm. The comparatively small Rochester real estate market in which Holly operates makes this fact doubly amazing.

Today, Holly's major ambition is imparting sound knowledge of business and good ethical principles to her children.

> **She always fostered in them the belief that you can do anything you want if you simply have clear goals in mind to get there and work hard to consistently meet them every single time.**

Holly's oldest daughter, Alixandra, was one of the country's top rated tennis players in her youth and now owns a very successful business in Chicago. Tori has followed in her mother's footsteps, and has recently relocated back to Rochester from Arizona, where she was a successful realtor. She is now full-time on Holly's team. Paul's business took off after seven long years of groundwork and is quite successful to this day.

When asked about how she achieved her unqualified success, Holly of course cited the power of goal setting and the willingness to stick to a plan over the long term. She also indicates the importance of something that her father once told her:

"If you retire too young, that's a dangerous thing..."

Holly asserted that because of this advice, she was open to changing her entire paradigm when the time was right. Going from a stay-at-home mother to an active member of the workforce certainly qualifies as a life-altering change, and it's also something that couldn't have been done without adhering to such a credo. Yet for Holly, who had the ability to see it through to the end, it's a gamble that's paid off big time.

Lauren Dixon

CEO of Dixon Schwabl

"Forget conventionalisms; Forget what the world thinks of you stepping out of your place; think your best thoughts, speak your best words, work your best works, looking to your own conscience for approval."
Susan B. Anthony

Lauren Dixon's turning point came about as a result of her being in a desperate situation; and quite literally asking herself how she was going to get out of it.

Put in a scenario where she basically had no choice but to succeed in the advertising industry, Lauren went right to the source and set up interviews with local businesses that made use of advertising agencies. She interviewed individuals from ten large businesses, ten mid-sized businesses, and ten small businesses. She asked each of them a set of questions, designed to give her a critical perspective of how the business of advertising was perceived from the side of the companies that pay for it. Among these was a query regarding which things companies most disliked about the advertising agencies they had worked with in the past.

To her surprise, Lauren found herself hearing literally the same answers repeated back at her over and over again. All thirty of the people she interviewed came back to her with the same three things that they hated about working with advertising agencies: they charged too much for production, they didn't care about the businesses they were working for, and their actual fees were always far in excess of their estimates, sometimes nearly one-hundred times as much! Lauren saw an opportunity for success and seized upon it, making it her personal mission to both avoid these pitfalls and fill the niche left open by others in the industry. Before we get into how she did that, a bit of background information.

Lauren was the first in her family to go to college. She attended Kent State and pursued a degree in broadcasting that stemmed from her desire to connect with people. She did well there and formed many of the convictions about how to treat people that would color her approach to business later in life.

In April of 1987, Lauren found herself in something of a desperate situation. She was 31 years old and going through a divorce, with two children aged three and one and a half. She was looking to restart her life, but quickly ran into some setbacks. She had already spent many years in a career in broadcast advertising as a news anchor and as a local television sales manager. She had been looking for a change of pace when she found a promising career opportunity with the large communications company, TAFTS Broadcasting, based in Cincinnati. But just before she was set to move, her husband voiced concerns about her moving so far away with their children, and a court ultimately decided in his favor. In order to maintain the custody situation as it presently was, Lauren wasn't allowed to move outside of a 75 mile radius. By coincidence, when she left her job in broadcasting, she had signed an agreement to the effect that she wouldn't take a job in the same industry at any competing companies within a 75 mile radius!

Lauren suddenly found herself with no job, no prospects within her chosen profession, and two small children to take care of. Seeking solace from her father, Lauren was given the advice that she should try to own her own business in order to avoid similar situations in the future. Given that she had a strong background in advertising from her broadcast career already, Lauren decided to move in that direction and had the defining, eye-opening moment that we mentioned above. Based on what the companies she interviewed told her, she saw the opportunity and realized:

"These three things that they dislike with a passion can be my points of differentiation."

Having found her niche, Lauren got started. She deposited $22.11, the entirety of her savings, into a business account and set out to get a loan. She was put into contact with a local accountant, Jim Cohen, to discuss these matters. Meeting with Jim proved to be an eye-opening experience in and of itself; he had a grim warning to offer: 94% of businesses fail within their first year, and 96% of those that make it that far fail in the following year. Determined not to become one of these statistics, Lauren structured her business plan around Jim's advice and her commitment to the niche she had found.

It was a year marked by struggle. She worked out of her young son's nursery and saved every possible penny. She didn't redecorate the yellow duck wallpaper of the nursery. She didn't eat out. She didn't even buy underwear for an entire year. But in the end, it paid off. Having virtually no operating costs, she closed out her first year in the advertising business with 2 million dollars in billings. Quickly acquiring more and more accounts, the business really took off from there.

The proof of Lauren's success came in 1989, when she and her partner, new husband Mike Schwabl were awarded the distinction of being placed among the top 25 small businesses to work for in the entire United States. She attributes this success to her skills in team-building, her focus on employees, and of course her commitment to fulfilling the niche established by less thoughtful competitors.

When asked where she plans to go from here, Lauren indicates that wherever she goes, she hasn't forgotten her small-town roots. Born in a town of 200 people, she was instilled from birth with the values of a strong work ethic and the importance of charity. **Each year, she and her employees have given back 2800 hours of their time to charities in their community.**

On top of this admirable pursuit, she is constantly reinventing herself. Having already met with success in two careers, she feels confident that she could do it again, and some days considers building an entirely new business from new technology that has interested her. Whatever she does, it will undoubtedly be marked by the same commitment to fulfill peoples' desires in a caring and personal way, and to adhere to and fill a niche left by her competition that has made her current endeavor such a rousing success.

Rick Dorschel

CEO of The Dorschel Automotive Group

"In the swim of life, you can either decide to spend your time in the shallow end, or go out to the ocean."
Christopher Reeve

Like many of the most successful businessmen of the world, Rick Dorschel was strongly influenced by his family – his father in particular. Rick's father worked the family business of running an automotive dealership. From his youngest years, Rick remembers his father instilling him with a work ethic that would eventually go on to define his entire approach to business and also give him the edge required to attain the success that he has gone on to achieve.

When Rick was only six or seven years old, during his second year of school, he got his first job at his father's dealership. He worked on Saturdays, giving up the opportunity to play ballgames and engage in typical schoolboy activities with his friends, in order to learn the ropes of the industry. Starting with sweeping the floors, Rick would perform practically every job at the dealership, learning as much as possible about everything there was to know there.

Though he describes his father as a difficult person to get along with, due in large part to his staunch devotion to the family business, Rick still values the work ethic and perseverance that all of these experiences instilled in him.

Around this time, another event happened that would shape Rick's course in life, teaching him in a very direct fashion about the importance of perseverance and hard work.

In the fifth grade, he took up swimming lessons and had a completely miserable time of it. Rick was overweight at the time and the physically demanding sport brought him to exhaustion and ridicule rather than pleasure. However, he had already learned the basic principles of self-determination from his stints at the family business, and so he decided to stick with it, not abandoning the sport simply because it was difficult. As he phrases it, **"I never had a lot of talent, but I was good at perspiration."**

In time, this perseverance paid off and Rick lost weight, becoming much more adept at the sport of swimming, winning the respect and admiration of others, and boosting his own confidence in his convictions. Thus assured that hard work and determination could indeed work both professionally and personally, Rick redoubled his efforts and would soon experience the event that he now thinks of as his turning point.

After college, a stint in the U. S. Army and an engagement to his high school sweetheart, Nancy, Rick continued to work at his father's dealership. But before long, he began to express more of an interest in the managerial aspects of the business.

Confident that he could lead the business to new levels of success, Rick approached his father about buying the family business. He received a sound refusal.

The two of them would go back and forth for many years with Rick constantly making offers and arguing all the reasons as to why he would be the best choice to run the company. His father, however, would not be moved. Seeing that there was little he could do to advance in his current situation, Rick approached a competing dealership and began to talk with them about employment. Rick took this a step further and even began to envision what would happen if he were to make use of this new company to actually buy out his father's business.

This was enough to get his father's attention. Not wanting the dealership to go out of the family, he approached Rick and uttered the life-altering words, "I'll give you an opportunity."

That opportunity turned out to be all that Rick needed. He continued to work with the family dealership, taking on roles of increasing responsibility until the point that he eventually purchased the business from his father. Thanks in large part to his powerful work ethic and sense of determination, Rick has guided the company to unprecedented levels of success. Today, he is one of the top auto dealers in the entire Rochester region, enjoying a massive share of the market that also makes him one of the most successful businessmen in the region, period.

Although he does have a certain flair for business, Rick stresses that this was something he learned purely from experience on the job. The real reason behind his success, as he tells it, is his commitment to the ideas of hard work.

As Rick likes to say, **"if you can't out think them, you can out work them."**

The determination that kept him going to the dealership instead of having fun with his friends, the determination that kept him going to his swimming lessons in spite of the difficulties he had there, the determination that kept him in negotiations with his reluctant father about taking over the family business, this was the exact same determination that drove his business towards a level of success beyond what anyone had ever imagined.

Rick refers to this type of thinking as having unlimited belief patterns. To him, **the idea of under-setting goals and not pressing forward at all times is self-defeating and self-limiting**. Rick believes that he fully realizes his potential only by truly believing that there are no limits whatsoever to his forward motion other than his own willingness to work hard. Certainly, this belief pattern has brought him success in his own life, and brought him to the turning point, the opportunity that changed everything for him.

Today Rick could easily retire, but chooses not to. To him, retiring would be implicitly admitting an end to the meteoric rise of his business. He continues to work so that he can continue to break barriers and push the boundaries of success. When asked about where he wants to go in the future, Rick holds true to some of his father's principles, revealing the incredible degree of influence that the man still holds over his life.

Having invested so much into the family business, Rick has no desire to see it go into the hands of others. As such, he is currently in talks to transition the business to his son-in-law, continuing the trend of Dorschel's success in the automotive dealership business for yet another generation.

All things told, the secret of Rick's success is a combination of influences. There are the values he received from his father, the importance of hard work, and then the experiences of his own life that concretely showed him how those values could be applied to life in a way that brought forth real results. With this as the foundation, his hard work did the rest to bring him to where he is today.   Rick's success is an incontrovertible statement to the power of belief and the success it can bring if one applies one's convictions to one's life, unrelentingly.

Turning Points

Michael Frame

Managing Broker CB Richard Ellis

"We don't see things as they are; we see things as we are."
Anais Nin

Michael Frame's turning point is the event that helped instill in him the critical element of his success: his ability to see events and people from a series of perspectives, through as broad a lens as possible, and then apply the lessons learned to his own life.

When Michael was still in college, he had the unique opportunity to spend semesters abroad in any number of different countries. Wanting something that was truly unique, he opted to spend one of those semesters in Kenya, where he had what he describes as a truly life altering experience. He spent time there with families whom he described as truly disadvantaged, those without even enough to eat. Further, he was shocked to discover that little was thought to be strange about a man arriving nearly two hours late to a meeting! Instead of allowing himself to be frustrated by these matters, however, Michael sought to integrate them into his own way of thinking, to come to appreciate and admire the culture he was experiencing and to put what it had to offer to work in his own life. **This ability to draw value out of any situation he encounters and use it to color the way he views the world** is what has kept Michael on top of his game all these years and led him to the great success that he enjoys today.

His parents had instilled in him many important values such as a strong work ethic and the necessity of treating people kindly while relating to them in a personal way. Michael recalls being taught by his father to look everyone directly in the eye and to give a good, deal-closing handshake at only five years old.

During his first years of college, Michael worked at R. P. Meyers, a construction company, where he dug ditches during the day. This was a physically demanding job that had him drenched in sweat and dirt, but he valued the experience tremendously. He was able to interact with the other workers there, to fit in as one of them, and of course to learn from them.

In line with his belief that the most important thing in business (indeed, in life) is seeing things from a broad perspective, Michael studied psychology in college, and it was during this time that he made his fondly remembered trip to Kenya. That was an experience he valued so much that he made a vow to travel the world in five years time, to visit as many countries as possible, and to learn as much from the world as it was willing to offer. He committed himself to this goal by telling friends, family, and even strangers that after college he was going to work for a company to save the necessary money to pay for the trip and achieve his goal. By the time five years had passed, he met his future wife Sue and kept true to his word by setting off on his trip around the globe with her.

Visiting innumerable locales throughout Europe, Asia, and the South Pacific, Michael was on the road an entire year, living out of a backpack. To this day, he credits the lessons he learned during this time as the singular key to his great success. In his own words, "If you had a trophy shelf in life of all the things you had accomplished, doing what I did then still has top shelf status".

Returning at last from his travels and having learned as much about the world and humanity as he possibly could, Michael was at last ready to put his skills into practice. He worked for Xerox Learning Systems based in New England, training literally hundreds of people from all walks of life and from all areas of the country to hone their communication skills, which highlighted Michael's interest in helping them to reach higher levels of achievement.

In 1989 Michael wanted to move back to Rochester to raise his young family, even though it was a time when many people were moving out of the area. Bringing along his somewhat reluctant but supportive wife, Michael secured a job with Wilmorite, a real estate company in Rochester. He describes this experience as working by himself, stationed out of an empty office building in downtown that was furnished with little more than a phone and phone book. Here he was expected to make it work. Make it work, he did. Drawing upon his array of people skills and psychological knowledge, Michael set out building up a base of customers, often through door to door salesmanship, and soon had established himself as a successful player in the real estate industry.

After 6 years at Wilmorite, he was looking for a new challenge when he was hired into a real estate development company by Daniel Murphy. Daniel told him that although he was not the most qualified candidate on paper, he saw in Michael the potential to develop into exactly the kind of insightful employee they were desperate for. Eventually, they opened the CB Richard Ellis office in Rochester. Today, he continues to move in the directions that interest him by offering commercial real estate brokerage and consulting services.

Asked about his success, Michael firmly states that it is impossible to separate his professional life from his personal one. Nearly the entirety of his personal life has been devoted to the pursuit of knowledge of other people and cultures and Michael indicates that this single characteristic has made all of the difference in how he approaches professional matters; it's what allowed him to carve out his own niche. By adhering to the principles that he was personally passionate about, Michael has been able to bring his personal philosophy to the field of real estate; he has this to say:

> **"When working with others to help them to address their needs, most people ask questions that begin with *what*, rarely do they follow up with questions that start with *why*, that is to understand the importance of the *motivation* behind what they said, what they are thinking and what they are trying to accomplish".**

Motivated by a sincere desire to understand and appreciate other people for what they have to offer, Michael has proven that personal philosophical beliefs and success in professional matters indeed go hand in hand, and that the human element of business should never, ever be overlooked because that's the largest part of any issue in life.

<u>Andy Gallina</u>

President of Gallina Development

"Imagination is more important than knowledge."
Albert Einstein

Andy Gallina remembers his turning point quite clearly and says that the shock waves from that moment have spread throughout his entire life.

> *He recalls one afternoon when he was in the eighth grade, in a room in his father's basement that measured no greater than 8 x 8 feet. He was practicing lacrosse, a sport for which he had great passion, by throwing a ball at the wall and catching it. Somewhat hypnotized by the rhythm of the ball, he began to formulate a vision for his future. Stemming from his passion for lacrosse and his natural desire to be a good player, Andy made a*

> **vow to himself to make the All Upstate lacrosse team and to be published in their magazine: The Guide to Upstate Lacrosse. Although he wasn't the fastest, the quickest, or the strongest player, Andy did have two solid advantages; his desire to succeed, and more importantly, the goal that gave him such a clear image of achievement.**

During his years at Irondequoit high school, Andy did go on to meet this goal. He set a school record in goals scored and began playing Varsity in his junior year. In his senior year, he succeeded in making the All Upstate team and saw his name in print in their magazine. Further, Andy became the first person in Rochester to be named to the All American Lacrosse Team. In his college years, Andy would go on to meet with success as a part of Brown University's lacrosse team. Though Andy's ambition never was to become a professional lacrosse player, he says that **the experience of setting a goal and systematically meeting it through careful planning and hard work was absolutely integral to his success in business**. The lessons learned here have gone on to influence his entire career, and would ultimately bridge the gap between his two passions: sports and real estate.

From his youngest years, family has always been a major influence in Andy Gallina's life. He recalls learning moral and philosophical values such as honesty from his mother, who immigrated to the United States from Italy at the age of 4. He learned more practical matters such as a strong work ethic from his father, who was a homebuilder in the area. When Andy was only five, his father brought him to a job site and had him help by pounding nails. This lesson in work ethic and knowing that he contributed to the valuable finished product of a house went a long way towards helping teach the young Andy the value of hard work. Later, when his uncle's house was being built, Andy was so eager to help that he was once again given the assignment of pounding nails. He was somewhat overzealous with this assignment, filling an entire board with nails packed head to head, and to this day it remains an anecdote that the entire family remembers fondly.

Perhaps stemming from his father's involvement with homebuilding, Andy went on to earn a degree in engineering at Brown University. As graduation approached, he saw his friends submitting applications and interviewing with employers from all across the country. His professors expected him to do the same, but Andy says he never particularly felt as if he belonged in any of the same establishments that his friends were so eager to get into. And so instead of languishing after college, his father insisted that he occupy his time by helping out with the family business. My Dad said, "Go ahead and take a week off, then let's get going". From there, Andy rather naturally fell into that line of work. He recalls an initial shock that he had just earned a college degree and was suddenly out slinging mud and sweating in the sun, but ultimately the values that his father and mother had helped instill in him won out, and he realized that he was doing what he loved. He describes it:

> **"Having the ability to visualize a project and follow it to fruition has brought me great satisfaction and reward."**

Throughout his career with his father's business, Andy still held on to the practice of setting goals and systematically working to achieve them. It was through these means that he became a homebuilder, just like his father, before branching out into the commercial real estate market. After some years in the business he met his wife Karen through a blind date, and she influenced him in his success to branch out into philanthropic gestures and to give back to the community. Andy recalls that while helping out one's loved ones was always a strong value in his family growing up, it wasn't until he met Karen that he learned the benefit of applying these values to a broader range. At this point, all of the influences that would shape Andy's life were firmly in place.

Almost as a matter of natural progression, Andy went on to develop what would be the ultimate culmination of all his influences and passions. Having learned about the concept of flex space soon after graduation, Andy expanded this concept to his native city of Rochester, bringing with it all the know-how for how to sustain a niche business in a crowded market. As the defining values of his life began to come together, Andy developed a grand vision for a business that would offer a service like no other to the sports-loving people of his city, and he knew that he had to take the chance. Combining his love for sports, philanthropy and building, Andy created the Total Sports Experience, or TSE, an indoor Rochester facility, where individuals can go to play just about any sport imaginable all year round. The Total Sports Experience afforded the citizens of Rochester the ability to practice their sport, or just remain active, even throughout the somewhat harsh winters for which Rochester is famous.

The Total Sports Experience is a very successful venture for Andy Gallina and his family and is a source of pride. Suddenly finding himself one of Rochester's most successful entrepreneurs, Andy would continue to give back to the community with his wife's influence. Together the two of them have a major impact on local organizations such as the MS Society, the Greater Rochester YMCA, The Al Sigl Center and Memorial Art Gallery to name but a few. In this way, as well as with his own children, Andy continues to impart his hard learned values of honesty, family, setting goals, and hard work.

From his high school career as an All Upstate lacrosse champion and All American, to being a successful contractor alongside his father and the staggering success of the Total Sports Experience, Andy Gallina's life can be looked at as one success after the other. And yet when he is asked for the secret to his success, Andy insists that there's really no secret at all. His belief is that: **Success is simply a matter** of making the most of everyday choices, setting goals, having the concrete plans to achieve them, and simply possessing a desire to achieve victory, no matter the odds.

Turning Points

Jane Glazer

Owner and President of QCI Direct

"I have become a 20 year overnight success."
Anonymous

Jane Glazer's rise to success has been marked by a gradual discovery of her own untapped potential and a willingness to defy the expectations that others had of her, in order to make the best for herself. She began life in an era when there were unwritten "rules" that women were expected to follow. Although nothing was stated explicitly, Jane says it was understood in her community that all women should aspire to one of three professions: teaching, nursing, or social services. Furthermore, none of these jobs should be thought of as a career; rather, they were simply seen as useful skills for a woman to possess in the event that something happened to her husband and she was left with a family to support.

Not knowing anything different, Jane consequently set out early in life to become a teacher. In the sixth grade, she found herself wanting for spending money, and so decided to open up her own day camp in her backyard for nursery school aged children. With the help of her father, she made up a brochure that advertised all the services she planned to render, such as providing the children with tutoring, snacks and a safe place to stay while their parents were busy. Today, Jane works in a much different profession, but she still has a framed copy of this brochure displayed in a place of honor. At the time, she saw the job as preparation for her teaching position. Nowadays, she realizes that she was really experiencing the first steps of her true calling in that she was setting up and advertising a business.

In the meantime, Jane did go on to graduate from the University of Buffalo and become a teacher, and married the equally successful Larry Glazer (whose story is covered elsewhere in this book). Described as coming from a somewhat liberated family that was "years ahead of the game," where even his mother worked hard at a job, Larry was among the first people to make Jane aware of her limited perception of herself. She first met him during a teaching stint at a summer camp where they were both working as counselors. In addition to meeting Larry, she also had the first of several formative experiences there, wherein others recognized her leadership potential. Because of her obvious qualities, she was asked to oversee a difficult cabin full of older girls that had proven to be too much for other counselors; an assignment that she handled quite efficiently.

Even while she was still under the grip of oppressive notions, Jane remained an active personality. After her children were born, she took time off from teaching to pursue her masters degree at Nazareth College. After receiving it, she planned to return to teaching but found that this decision was met with some incredulity by both her husband and her father. Why, they asked, did she feel she had to return to teaching when Larry's success afforded her the chance to do otherwise? However, Jane couldn't be talked into just sitting around at home. Larry recognized this about her and told her about a position at the publishing company that

Jane's father owned; a position putting together sales catalogs. Drawing on her early experiences from putting together lesson plans and syllabi as a teacher, Jane took to the job as a natural and became heavily involved with it, reaching a high level of expertise.

Coordinating a large group of people including artists, typists and merchandise suppliers, Jane felt she had at last found a job that challenged her true leadership and organizational abilities. However, when the publishing company was sold off years later, she found herself among the first to be let go. It was at that point that she was faced with a new decision. She simply didn't want to quit and give up the job that brought her so much gratification, so she decided to go into business for herself, putting together her own catalogs, accruing merchandise suppliers, and coordinating all of the sales. Working out of an empty room that she and Larry acquired, Jane worked hard at her new business, listening to Larry's advice, but still found herself losing money over the next seven years.

During that time, she also continued to experience remnants of the attitude that had kept her in the dark as to her potential for so long. When people found out she worked with her husband, they automatically made the assumption that she was his assistant, instead of acknowledging that she owned the business herself. This, combined with her lack of a profit after seven years, began to depress Jane and she started to wonder if she really had it in her after all. Around this time, she took a much needed vacation with another couple, and it was there that she had what she describes as her turning point.

After living a life of such revelation and drastic changes, what could possibly have been so life-altering at that point to qualify as a turning point to Jane? It was a simple comment made by the wife of the other couple on the vacation. When asked about why she thought her business wasn't turning a profit, Jane exclaimed that she had no idea

because she had been following Larry's advice to the letter. The other woman asked why she wasn't making her own decisions. Jane respected Larry's expertise as a salesman, but suddenly realized that after all, if it was to be her business, then she needed to be the one making the critical decisions, whether they succeeded or failed.

Returning from the vacation, Jane discussed the situation with Larry, and she became the driving force behind her business, making all decisions. Within a year, her penchant for leadership and organizational skills had allowed the business to turn its first ever profit and she moved into a bigger building. Things continued to grow, she continued to make excellent deals, and before long she was working out of a 250,000 square foot facility and commanding a workforce of over 150 employees. The company motto: **"Sure, No Problem"** is so ingrained as a company philosophy to take care of the customer, it is painted on the wall as soon as you enter the building.

Jane's road to success was a long one, full of personal discoveries, but she insists that her most important trait, the one most fundamental to her success, is that she's never stopped learning things about life, herself, or the nature of her business. As she says in her own words:

"This is a puzzle that you never get the final piece to."

Today, Jane's business continues to grow, and one need look no further than her workplace to find evidence of her ability to learn and grow. At the head of her workroom hangs a banner with the mantra, "Sure, no problem," a testament to Jane's ability to succeed despite all odds.

<u>Larry Glazer</u>

CEO of Buckingham Properties

"On the shores of hesitation, bleach the bones of those countless millions who on the edge of victory sat down to rest and resting died."
Winston Churchill

Though Larry Glazer describes his life's influences as being incredibly multi-layered, there was one point that truly qualifies as his turning point; an instant in which he was literally forced to either devise an innovative way to make his particular strengths and weaknesses work in the marketplace, or give up the real estate business altogether. This moment occurred in the early years of his business life, when, as Larry put it:

"We were working on gas fumes and credit cards..."

He and his partner, struggling to keep things afloat, had received an offer to buy a large office building in downtown Rochester, on Main Street. The two of them jumped at the chance, certain that this would be the big break they had been looking for. They met with the sellers and negotiated a favorable contract, even drew up papers and signed them. As they left, they were told to return in the morning when the out-of-town president of the company would return and put his own signature to the documents, finalizing the deal. Thinking that only a formality stood between them and the biggest deal of their lives, Larry and his partner celebrated, only to be called the next morning and told that the building was given to another buyer, a local competitor who had been given the remarkable advantage of looking at Larry's contract and making a slightly better offer.

This experience would be the turning point in Larry's career, the instant at which he realized he needed to apply his greatest strength - the strategic thinking of a chess player - to his career. Less than three months later, Larry and his partner made what they thought was a safe purchase of an industrial complex that had been occupied by Kodak for a number of years. When Kodak suddenly pulled up stakes and left, shortly after Larry purchased the property, he and his partner found themselves holding an expensive building with no occupants. Unable to sell the large facility as a whole, Larry realized that he had to play to his strengths.

He and his partner were experts at getting good deals when it came to buying real estate at a good value. With this in mind, he hit upon the innovative idea that has redefined his entire life and brought him his greatest successes; he would split the property into smaller parcels and rent out each one individually, thus turning one property (whose occupants could vacate at any moment) into countless smaller properties that served as more stable sources of income.

This type of strategic thinking was developed early in Larry's life and was the result of many different events and influences that stacked upon one another to make Larry the person he is today. As Larry was growing up, he constantly saw his father inventing new things. A very creative individual, Larry says that his father was actually a very insightful inventor who first created many of the things that we take for granted today, such as the idea of a coin-operated Laundromat, lanolin based hand creams, waterless hand soap, and silicon based ironing aides to name a few. However, in spite of his creativity, his father never had the business acumen to patent any of his creations, and so he never made a penny's profit from them. Watching his father's potential go to waste, Larry became frustrated and first realized the importance of strategic thinking and learning practical business skills.

Some time later, Larry took a job as a summer camp counselor, and it was there that he met his wife, Jane. Larry describes the influence Jane had over him as instrumental to his success. Evolving from his philosophy of careful strategic planning for the future, Jane helped Larry to understand that **one has instincts for a reason and that sometimes it's logical to listen to them.** Larry would go on after college to join her family's printing company, Great Lakes Press. While working there, he was contacted by an old friend Harold Samloff, who proposed the idea of he and Larry starting their own real estate practice. Bolstered by Jane's faith in him, Larry jumped at the chance and embarked down the path of his current career.

Even as his real estate business continued to expand, Larry continued to work with Great Lakes Press. When he reached the age of 35, however, he began to ask the question "do I want to stay in the family business or pursue the creativity of real estate development?" After a conversation with his father-in-law, Larry who by then had become co-CEO, decided to sell the business altogether to pursue real estate full time. Using the knowledge and strategic thinking he had learned from his real estate business, Larry was able to negotiate a very favorable deal when selling Great Lakes Press, and his father-in-law ended up being very pleased with how things turned out.

Since then, Larry's flair for thinking ahead and setting up solid plans for success has taken his real estate business to levels of achievement perhaps greater than he had ever envisioned. Nevertheless, as is fitting for a man with such diverse influences, Larry is always on the lookout for new ways to refine his ideas about business. For example, at the age of 38, Larry took up flying. As he tells it, the discipline required to learn this complicated new skill has taught him many new things that he's eager to apply to his business in the future. When all is said and done, this is perhaps Larry's greatest strength: the ability to see the big picture and draw helpful influences from literally any source, influences that make him a better thinker, a better businessman, and a more successful person.

Don Golini

President of QED Technologies

"So easy it seems once found, yet when unfound
most would have thought impossible."
John Milton

Don Golini remembers his turning point quite clearly, and while it's not exactly an instance of high drama as might be expected, it highlights the importance of individuals and small gestures that ironically defines Don's entire outlook.

The moment came when he was in his late teenage years, sitting in the driveway at his friend's house in his car, a 1972 Dodge Polara, listening to the Beatles. Influenced perhaps by the counter-culture ambience of their soundtrack, the discussion between Don and his friend turned to careers and joining the workforce; the debate was: do you want to work for money, or do you want to have a real passion for what you do? In a climate where many people viewed those two options as a strict

> **dichotomy, each one excluding the other, Don recognized that he wanted to succeed, but also needed to do so with passion. Without making compromises, he wanted to forge his own way and be recognized.**

Don's ambition to succeed in an area that he was passionate about was helped along no doubt by his home life and upbringing. His parents weren't wealthy, and both held down local 9 to 5 jobs in order to support the household; but they always put their faith in Don and gave him a very strong sense of self-confidence, leading Don to feel that there were quite literally no limits to what he was capable of achieving.

Needless to say, this "no limits" personality of Don's led to his taking interesting approaches to various challenges throughout his life. When he first entered college, Don enrolled in pre-med studies, but he wasn't exactly in the highest ranks as far as academics were concerned. Although he held his own in such a competitive field, Don's interest in engineering did eventually win out and he changed his major. Not wanting to settle for anything that could be termed "mundane", Don knew that he would want to pursue a unique specialty even within engineering - one that would satisfy his passions and set him apart from the crowd. So optical engineering it was.

After graduation, Don went to work at Itek Optical Systems as an engineer. He says that he chose this company not so much for the salary that he received there, but for the company's outstanding reputation in the industry. Thanks to Itek's somewhat liberal business structure and unique culture, Don not only received direct feedback on his work from all levels of the company, but he was also able to give feedback to anyone, regardless of their position or stature. At times, he even recalls giving his opinion directly to the CEO. This was a business model that greatly appealed to

Don and impressed him so much that he still refers to it when managing his own business today.

It was during this time that Don received something of a booster shot, reaffirming his belief that **pursuing one's passions works in tandem with the pursuit of success.** A much older co-worker by the name of Witkor Rupp knew a lot about optical manufacturing, and he told Don that if he were to specialize in such a rapidly growing and essential field, he would never find himself wanting for work. Rather, people would be crawling over one another to offer him jobs. The field really intrigued Don, and helped him put into clear belief his philosophy that passion and success go hand in hand. As he himself puts it:

> **"Spend ten years becoming an expert at something... if it can be differentiated and specialized, even better... because if you're the best at something, you can leverage that."**

Don received his master's degree in optical engineering and realized that his mentor's words had held true. His position at Itek was so secure that he could have worked there forever if he wanted to, but as Don tells it, he wanted more. Around this time, he happened to meet an Eastman Kodak executive by the name of Harvey Pollicove, who was working at the University of Rochester's Center for Optics Manufacturing. The two of them hit it off famously, and Don went to work for him for four years, learning more about the ins and outs of the optical industry. Drawing on his own personal beliefs about management, personal passions and a no-limit attitude, Don met with success in this field as well, but would again turn to something new after only four years.

At last drawing together all of his influences, Don finally found what he describes as his own way in life. Combining his commitment to his work and his personal passion (themselves one and the same), his self-confidence, his technical expertise in the field of optical engineering, and his strong beliefs in company culture held over from Itek, Don drew up his own business plan. Don went to his wife Tracey, to tell her that he wanted to start his own business and received her unwavering support and trust.   In 1996, he opened QED Technologies, a manufacturing company involved in optical technology and polishing.   It operated under Don's own personal convictions, with a mission statement emphasizing the importance of a highly diverse body of workers, each of whom are able to contribute their own individual passion and value.   Filling a real niche in the optical market, Don's company quickly met with great success. Today, QED is a market leader in the United States, but also has offices in Europe and Asia, surpassing even Don's own expectations.

When asked about the future, Don indicates, not surprisingly, that he wants to continue to do unique and unexpected things.   No matter what he does, however, he says he always intends to adhere to that fundamental premise of never divorcing passion from work and using that to develop an area of desirable technical expertise that has already brought him so far.

Tom Hassett

President of T & L Automatics

"Nobody will believe in you, unless you believe in yourself."
Liberace

Tom Hassett is an individual who has not only had a turning point, but a truly defining characteristic as well. Everything about Tom demonstrates the aggressive attitude and merciless pursuit of success that has gotten him so far, from his straightforward manner of speaking to the history that has helped define him.

Born into what might be called something of an underdog status, Tom was the youngest child in his family, despite being taller than average height (his present day stature is an imposing 6' 4"). In school, he routinely got poor grades despite constantly being told by his teachers how intelligent he was, and how he just simply wasn't working up to his potential. It was something of a precarious time for Tom, and in the 7th grade yearbook he was even voted most likely to be held back! Yet he viewed all of this with something of a

71

detached perspective, continuing to persevere. It wasn't until the 10th grade that he began to prove the suspicions of his teachers correct and get excellent marks. Tom indicates that, had they had modern-day diagnosis back then, he might very well have been told he had an attention deficit disorder. Why is any of this relevant? Because, quite simply, it demonstrates a critical fact about Tom: to never give up.

Tom did have a turning point, but it wouldn't occur until after he had graduated high school.

Despite being given the option to attend Rochester Institute of Technology, Tom chose to enter the Army. His ambition was to be a helicopter pilot, and though he met all the skill requirements for the position, he was eventually passed over for the job due to being too tall. Suddenly, he was relegated to an infantry position and found himself in a prime position to be shipped to Vietnam.

At first he wasn't too afraid, since he excelled at all of his physical tests and was a good soldier, but one day at his station in Fort Gordon, Georgia, Tom was given the opportunity to walk the wards of the Fort hospital and today can still recall hearing the moaning sounds of the wounded soldiers. He went to meet someone that was there, the brother of a family friend by the name of Fitzgerald, who had been to Vietnam and had come back wounded. Speaking with him terrified Tom, as he was easily able to imagine himself coming home to the same fate.

Suddenly faced with a realistic view of his prospects, Tom first adopted the aggressive salesmanship tactics that have taken him so far. Knowing that soldiers with certain qualities were in demand in the European theatre of Southern Germany, Tom began to do what was necessary to get transferred there, and thus to stay out of Vietnam. He certainly possessed the skills that were in demand, and before long, he says, his natural skills as an assertive and aggressive leader began to emerge. He found himself actually liking his job and he showed such a fine command of leadership skills that he was even asked to command soldiers of higher ranks than himself on several occasions. Having taken control of the circumstances around him, Tom walked away with a new outlook on things that would go on to define the rest of his life:

"You can't let life run you, you have to go out and run your life."

Upon returning from Europe, Tom's leadership qualities proved to be a powerful asset to him professionally. He first went to work at a business his father was a partner in as a night foreman. Before long, he was advanced to the position of day foreman and expanded to other jobs as well, in an attempt to gain as much experience as he could. At this same time, Tom met his wife and began to attend school at the Rochester Institute of Technology. Growing dissatisfied with the conditions of working under others, he decided to start his own company along with his father. To put things in perspective, this means he was working two jobs at once, developing his own business and attending school at the same time. Without the aggressive mentality, penchant for self-organization and leadership skills that he had so come to value, it seems practically impossible that Tom would have succeeded.

But succeed he did. Though his manufacturing company, T & L Automatics, got off to something of a slow start, Tom was there to see it through. Knowing fully how well he could do any job that was given to him, Tom was not afraid to make "cold calls". This means that he would often drive upwards of four to five hours to Cleveland in order to call upon the employees at Parker, a very large company, in an attempt to make contacts there. Due to his persistence, he did eventually make an impression upon them. Once his foot was in the door, Tom says it was his reputation that did the talking. T & L Automatics was able to do any job they were given in a professional and straightforward manner, thanks to Tom's leadership, and as such it began to be said of Tom **"if he tells you he's going to do it, it will get done."**

Subsequently, he got lots of business with Parker, and even more through the positive word of mouth generated by the professional reputation he had built up with them.

As one might expect, the lesson of the importance of selling oneself with an aggressive and unrelenting attitude has not diminished in importance over time with Tom. Even after having met with great success in his business, he continues to look to the future. Sleeping a mere three hours a night, Tom uses every spare moment he can to think about things, to analyze where he's come from and where he's going. When asked about the future of his business, he has something very blunt to say:

"If you don't grow, you're dead."

Intending to stay in the game for the long run, Tom constantly redefines the paradigm of T & L Automatics, having recently hired a new director of marketing, and constantly pushing his way into manufacturing new types of products and figuring out the best ways to work with them. Always moving forward, always confident and always stressing his strengths, Tom Hassett has struck upon a surefire recipe for success, and it's one that he recommends to others wholeheartedly.

Dan Hogan

CEO of Crane Hogan Structural Systems, Inc.

"Don't give up, don't ever give up."
Jim Valvano

Dan Hogan's turning point would occur only after he thought he was well on his way into a promising career. What at first seemed like an experience that would totally derail his plans and set him back indefinitely, instead gave him the opportunity to reevaluate his entire perspective on life, giving him an all new approach that enabled him to achieve the great success he currently enjoys.

Dan grew up in a fairly idyllic childhood, with a good family and good friends as he recalls it. He always assumed that he would secure a white collar job, as that was the sort of thing that was expected at the time. He attended Le Moyne College after an early graduation from high school and finished in 1968, earning a degree in Accounting.

Before he could choose between attending law school or entering the workforce, Dan was drafted. Faced with the prospect of joining the Army, he instead heeded some advice that he received from a Navy Recruiter, and joined the Navy's Seabees Construction Battalions instead for a two year enlistment. After basic training, Dan was sent to

Vietnam on a tour of duty that lasted for nine months.

He had initially dreaded the experience, but in many ways he now regards it as one of the most important formative experiences of his life. His service with the Seabees and his time in the field has taught him values such as focus, responsibility, maturity and perhaps most importantly, it taught him the value of specialization and channeling his ambition towards a specific goal that needed to be filled. Witnessing the way the military was organized, with each person doing a related critical job and doing it well, Dan realized the importance of teamwork and finding a niche.

When he returned from the service, he was 24 years old. He was eager to find a new identity for himself and get back to work to make use of his new skills, but he found that the subtle changes imposed upon his life in a war zone had left him well behind his contemporaries. Dan realized that all kinds of technological and procedural changes had taken place in the white collar game, that he was just now experiencing for the first time.

"I was two or three years behind ... I had to ratchet it up in order to make up for lost time, and I was also eager to use my new energy and focus rather than my old complacent college perspective."

He began to look for a new job, interviewing for both accounting positions and construction positions, feeling that his two extremes of experience made him suitable for either line of work. In the end, however, he felt that accounting would offer better opportunities, so he resolved to take that avenue. He interviewed with a company and quickly secured a job with a national accounting firm. But after only two days, he began to rethink whether this was what he wanted to do with his life. Convinced he had taken the wrong direction, he resigned from the accounting job and scheduled another interview for a late Friday afternoon with a construction company located in Syracuse, NY. He was hired immediately, and they asked him to start that evening and work the weekend. This was in November 1970, and the firm was Congel-Reuter Inc., the parent company of the Pyramid Companies.

It wasn't long until Dan figured out how Congel-Reuter's culture worked. He began working fifteen hour days, six days a week. Before long, he was noticed and he began to step up his game even more. Dan worked from 7 in the morning until 10 or 11 at night, stopping only then because he was running up on sixteen hours, and it was against company policy to accrue more than two days' pay on only one shift. During his second week at the job, Dan worked 28 hours straight estimating a construction project.

In Congel-Reuter's training program, Dan loved to be sent out into the field where he could demonstrate his work ethic. He would work hard, barely sleeping, for 2-4 hour periods at a time. Of the 80 people he began the program with, Dan was one of maybe ten who survived it successfully. After about six months of working with Congel-Reuter, they gave him the opportunity to oversee a job all on his own, with the only guideline being a certain monetary return that he was expected to earn during that time. Dan not only succeeded, he tripled the expectations of the company. Dan acknowledges that he had a great team working under him, but it's clear that this experience had a powerful effect on him: the belief that someday he could start his own company.

Eventually, the management at Congel-Reuter began to go in a new direction. After two and a half years with them, two of their partners who were also dissatisfied with the new direction broke off to start their own company, and made Dan an offer to come along with them and receive a 6.5% share in the company. Dan eagerly did so and found himself energized by getting out from under the authority of his first employer. He enjoyed the newfound freedom, and although he and the other two partners had a parting of ways after two years, the experience gave him the focus and courage to start his own business. Finally, Dan thought, he had found what he was meant to do.

Drawing upon his ability to focus his convictions towards an objective and his knowledge that a niche is crucial for success, Dan started his own company performing specialized coating, concrete projects and rehabilitation jobs on parking garages in the city of Rochester. Whereas other companies would simply replace failing structures at massive costs, Dan used the expertise he had acquired throughout all his years in the industry to develop a better means to repair rather than replace. This gave him a significant edge over the competition and to this day, he still remains one of the most successful contractors in the area. He later expanded his niche to performing his similar structural rehabilitation services on dams and bridges, to name a few; something that at the time no one else anywhere offered.

As Dan has gotten older, he says that the most rewarding part of his job is watching young people like himself come into the business and helping them to develop their skills and gain direction in their life. His own two sons have been successful on their own; his oldest opened his own engineering firm in Boston and his youngest is an entrepreneurial finance major. No matter which direction his sons or the young people working for him want to take, Dan is always quick to remind them about the importance of having the ability to focus on something, and finding your own niche where you are able to perform better than anybody else. As Dan likes to say, "**self satisfaction and fulfillment equals success."**

John Holtz

President of Holtz House of Vehicles

"The world is full of abundance... all you have to do is ask."
Anonymous

John Holtz has always known what it was he wanted; moreover, he's always known that in order to get it he would have to earn it and also ask for it. When he was a young man, even as far back as thirteen years old, John knew that he wanted to one day run his own business. At the young age of 28, John realized that dream in a chain of events that serves today as his turning point: a time when he gave himself concrete proof that all his convictions and all his ideas about business and how to approach it were sound, and destined to bring him great success.

When John was only 19 his father died. In the ensuing process of taking care of arrangements and the like, he decided to finish his education at the Rochester Institute of Technology. Perhaps more significantly, though, it was here that he would go

79

to work for his brother at a car dealership while putting himself through school. In only a short period of time, he realized that he could do more than simply work at a dealership; he had the knowledge, the passion and the drive to own one entirely for himself, thereby reaching his goal of owning his own business.

John began stowing away his savings from his job at the dealership, and before long he had saved up roughly ten thousand dollars, a sum that he says accounted for his entire life savings at the time. That in hand, he set out to find a dealership that he could buy, and true to his ideals of simply working for and asking for what one deserves, he went about it in the most straightforward and direct manner possible. John literally went from door to door, visiting all the dealership owners in the area and asking if they had any interest in selling to him. After a handful of false starts, he was able to make the down payment on a Honda motorcycle store, which he took over and began to run. It wasn't quite a full dealership, but it was a major step in the right direction and he was, after all, running his own business for the time being.

Most important of all is what the success meant to John.

Having long held to the notion that **all that stands between most individuals and their success is their unwillingness to step forward and ask for the chances that they deserve**, John had used these exact principles to seek out the job that he wanted.

When it paid off and he became the owner of the Honda motorcycle store at age 25, John knew that his convictions were solid. He resolved that they would stay with him throughout the rest of his life and career.

The motorcycle store was a success and John was able to generate substantial profits in just a short amount of time. He remembers the constant flurry of buyers during the spring and summer, as well as the fact that they tended to dry up somewhat throughout the winter. After all, who would want to ride a motorcycle during the Rochester winter? Faced with the prospect of inactivity several months out of the year, it wasn't long before John was looking for something more, and went back to hunting for dealerships with the help of his newly earned savings.

Again, he put in the footwork and went door to door. Before long, he had heard Honda wanted to put a store in the Henrietta, NY area. John's knowledge of the local area, derived in large part from his constant footwork, gave him the advantage. He knew of a local furniture store with attached land that would be perfect, and looked to buy it. Thanks to his persistence, John once again had succeeded; a deal was brokered, he purchased the furniture store, contacted Honda and found that they were delighted to offer him the area dealership. At the time, he was only 28 and already living his dream.

Of course, hard times would eventually come knocking on John's door, but this was nothing that he couldn't handle. In the 1990's, just after the business boom of the 80's, John had a total of sixteen dealerships under his name. What had been an advantage just a few years prior was now suddenly a liability and business was going down sharply. John knew that if he didn't do something soon, the possibility of hard times would soon fall on him. Not content to let that happen, he went back on the pavement, going door to door to local competing dealers, seeking to buy them out, always with his simple, straightforward approach. He kept this up, making purchases of strategic importance until his ends were achieved.

When he was done, John found himself the sole provider in town for high end automobiles. Anyone in the area who wanted a BMW, Porsche, Mercedes or any other car of that type would have to come to him. He had dramatically decreased his number of franchises, while at the same time establishing a niche for himself that would ensure his future success, and he had done it all by following his core philosophy.

That philosophy is something that John takes very seriously. When he was going through the trials of the early 90's, he became an ardent follower of Tony Robbins and attended several of his seminars. At those, he performed the stunt that further imbued him with self-confidence as it has for many of Robbin's followers: walking across a bed of hot coals, barefoot. Asked to expound upon his belief system, John had this to say:

> **"If you can walk on hot coals, is there anything you can't do?"**

Today, he's one of the most successful auto dealers in the region and continues to increase his business through the same old means that got him where he is in the first place. Although John isn't entirely certain of where he wants to take his operations in the future, he's confident that no matter where he goes, he'll achieve great success in whatever he does.

John's success is a clear example of how **one's outlook on life and one's philosophy can be directly tied in to one's business strategy**. Philosophy needn't be a matter of abstracts, but rather something that puts one's feet on the ground, moving in a solid direction, with great purpose and intent. This is how it was for John, and his commitment to unrelentingly pursuing his goals has made all the difference in his life, forming the structure for his great success.

Ray Hutch

CEO Synergy Global Solutions

*"If you don't set goals for yourself, you are doomed to
work to achieve the goals of someone else."*
Anonymous

Ray Hutch is an individual who learned very early on the
value of hard work, or as he puts it, that he was in control of
his own destiny.

*When he was 12 years old, Ray became enamored
with the notion of owning a racing bike. His
parents were receptive to the idea, but knowing
that it would make him value the possession quite a
bit more and consider the purchase more carefully,
they told him that he had to raise the money
himself. Inspired by ads in the back of the comic
books that he so loved to read, he discovered how
to make a profit by acting as a door to door
salesman for business cards and stationery. Ray
signed up with the company and went to work, and*

> **within one year he had raised the money necessary to purchase the bike of his dreams. Reflecting on this experience, Ray learned how to run a small business.**

Despite his early success with sales, Ray really had no idea what he wanted to do with his life, except that he had no real desire to sell life insurance as his father did. In his last days of high school he spoke with a guidance counselor, who looked over his academic records and advised him to become an engineer. At the time, Ray had no idea what an engineer even was, but having no better ideas himself decided to follow the counselor's suggestion and went on to Cornell University. After spending some time there, however, he realized he was merely "wasting his time" and had no real interest in the material being covered. He moved back closer to home, and finished his education at Trinity College, graduating in 1963. Soon thereafter, he took a job with IBM, but due to obligations from both the military and his family, he was unable to devote the time and attention that the demanding career required and they let him go. Convinced that the problem was with his lack of a real interest in the field of engineering, he asked them for a transfer to the sales department, but the company ultimately declined.

Feeling somewhat defeated and still not certain of what he wanted to do with his life, Ray took a job with Travelers Insurance Company. Though he had been certain earlier that this was an industry he definitely didn't want to enter, he stayed there while his wife, Erika, finished school. He asked Travelers to send him to a small city, so that he could raise his family in a community small enough that they would feel they could really make a difference there. Travelers instead ended up sending him to Chicago, of all places. Ray soon took another job with a company in the information systems business and was transferred to Rochester. There, he finally found the close-knit but modern community that he had been longing for. However, the company soon sold out, and the acquiring company wanted Ray to move to a larger city, while he wanted to stay in a small town to raise his family.

It was at this point that Ray recalled the success he'd had raising the money for his bike as a child, and resolved that once again he would become the master of his own fate. In his own words:

> **"I wanted to control my own destiny. I realized that, having been moved around by GE, IBM, Travelers... none of them had fulfilled my goals. The only way I could control my own destiny was to work for myself, to own my own business."**

Determined to create the life he wanted for himself and his family, Ray decided to open his own business. He knew his strong point lay in sales, but in an effort to differentiate himself and create his own niche, he wanted to combine that with the technical expertise he had learned in college and from working at IBM. Therefore, the business he established was one that resold access to university mainframe server computers for private use when they weren't being used. This at a time when owning a computer was well beyond the reach of most people. In fact, when Ray bought his own computer for use in his business, it cost him nearly $100,000, probably the equivalent to a million dollar machine in today's terms.

For the first 18 months, Ray focused on building up his business. He lived off savings and didn't take a salary during that entire period. What kept him going was the knowledge that he was in control of everything that was happening and that he could do it where he wanted: in the small community of Rochester, where he really felt he and his family could make a difference.

Ray's business was a success. By combining his salesmanship with his niche expertise, he was able to provide a service that no one else was offering, and his business began to grow by leaps and bounds. When 1987 rolled around and the price of personal computers began to drop to affordable levels, Ray wasn't caught off-guard; he simply altered the nature of his business, to sell the machines themselves and integrated this with software and network services. Once again, he was capitalizing both on his skills and on his knowledge.

Having achieved such great success, Ray is living the life he's always wanted to live, bringing up his family in a community where they try to make all the difference they can. And make a difference they do. Ray tries to give back to the community of Rochester in any way he can. One way he's done this is through once again exploiting his passions and personal interests. An avid swimmer in his spare time, Ray funded the non-profit organization QUAD A and the Eastside YMCA, to teach local children how to swim. Since its inception, that organization has taught more than 3000 kids to swim, improving the quality of their lives.

The story of Ray's turning point is a simple one, but its power lies in that simplicity.

> As Ray has shown, **the value of a single moment in one's youth cannot be underestimated, nor the power of combining one's true talents with the technical demands of the marketplace and the time one lives in.**

By simply doing what he loves and what he is good at, Ray has achieved his goals and made himself the master of his own destiny.

<u>Mike Jones</u>

CEO of Clover Capital Management

"Make the most of yourself, for that is all there is of you."
Ralph Waldo Emerson

The secret to Mike Jones' success lies in the influence that others in his life had over him during particularly impressionable moments of his life. From an early age, Mike was privileged to know several admirable individuals who he developed great relationships with, and who each had something to teach him. Sometimes in the form of direct advice and other times just in the form of acting as an inspiration to him, the lessons they imparted would form the turning points of Mike's life and set him on the path to become the success that he is today.

The first of Mike's turning points came in the form of his childhood family physician, Dr. Park Horton. Mike grew up in an incredibly small town of only about 800 people, so he got a chance to know the inhabitants there fairly well. The one who stood out the most to Mike was the local physician, Dr.

Horton, who would come to exercise a great deal of influence over Mike's development. As Mike saw the respect the physician commanded as he traveled around town making house calls with his black bag, he realized that in many ways, everyone in the town depended on Dr. Horton; he *was* the town in some sense.

Mike admired this about Dr. Horton and decided that he wanted to emulate that level of importance in his own life. He began to cultivate an interest in the healthcare field, and when the time eventually came for Mike to attend school, this is the path he chose. He went off to college with the intention of becoming an optometrist. It was there that he met not only his future wife, but also the second person to have a major influence on his life.

> *Professor Joel Thinnes was one of the youngest professors at Mike's junior college and as such, had a great deal of rapport with the students, especially Mike. One day he questioned Mike about what plans he had for his future, and when Mike replied that he wanted to become an optometrist, which was a very respectable trade, Thinnes replied that Mike had disappointed him. Previously, Mike had heard nothing but praise over his choice in career, and was shocked at this sudden reversal. When questioned further, Thinnes indicated that the reason for his response was that optometry was a field that would be easy for a person of Mike's intellectual capabilities. He wanted Mike to challenge himself with something more demanding he said, and questioned why he didn't take his studies further and become an ophthalmologist. "Reach for more," was his motto.*

Mike gave this some thought. Thinnes continued his encouragement, even to the point of taking him to visit other college campuses where Mike could finish his undergraduate degree. The insistence paid off and Mike eventually enrolled at the University of Rochester, where he studied pre-medicine.

In order to get the most out of his studies, Mike took a part time job in the emergency department at Strong Memorial Hospital, where he would get to work alongside doctors and assist in basic clinical duties in order to gain valuable experience. It would be an eye-opening experience for Mike, as it revealed to him the less glamorous side of the medical profession. Working amid the stress and trauma of the emergency room brought Mike to the conclusion that medicine was not the field for him after all.

The change in career plan did not dim his respect for his two mentors. Mike continued to see the value in their lessons. He hadn't admired Dr. Horton simply because he was a doctor, but rather because he was a central figure in his community - someone who anybody could turn to and who helped to get things done. Likewise, Thinnes had meant well by pushing Mike to challenge himself, and even if he didn't come to accept the particular profession of medicine, the lesson to **reach for more and not be satisfied with what was easily attainable** was a valuable one that he intended to carry with him.

Still quite young, and now with no particular plans for what to do with his life, Mike became engaged to his girlfriend; but right after they announced their plans, her father suffered a major heart attack. Wanting to help out, Mike took over control of the ailing man's real estate business, intending to run it until he got better. Using the skills he had learned from his mentors, together with his own ambition and perseverance, Mike began to excel in the real estate market. Mike gained new confidence from the realization that he was able to succeed in business, and began to push his ambitions to still further limits.

After his wife's father recovered, Mike applied for a job as a research analyst for an investment firm and found that the position was one that was perfectly suited for him in every way. Here, he was able to help people with their investment issues, similar to how Dr. Horton helped them with health issues. Also, his longstanding studies in the hard sciences had made him perfectly suited for the analytical aspects of the job, something that kept him constantly challenged and striving for more.

Eventually, Mike would build even further on his investment career. With a coworker by the name of Geoff Rosenberger, they started their own firm, Clover Capital. Now he performed the same service, analyzing the stock market and investing people's money for them in profitable ways. After a slow start where he found people reluctant about handing over their funds to someone so young, Mike and Geoff's company took off and today, Mike enjoys a level of success beyond what he ever would have imagined if not for the influence of his mentors.

The ultimate value of Mike's turning points and the lessons that he has been taught seems to be that **one must be ambitious and aim for the top, but one must also do what one loves**. As Mike himself puts it:

"I think that there's no substitute for hard work. It's impossible to work hard at something you don't like, though. So find something that you do like and work as hard as you can at it."

Furthermore, Mike's turning points have left him with the continual urge to reach higher and higher. Thanks to the influence of his mentors, this desire to go higher is so ingrained in Mike that he says he is not fearful of obstacles. Rather, when confronted with difficulty, his natural response is just to embrace the challenge and get to work to find a way to overcome it rather than to worry about it. It's certain that this confident, "strive for the best" approach has contributed greatly to Mike's amazing success in his field.

Turning Points

<u>Dick Kaplan</u>

President and CEO of Pictometry

*"Nothing in the world can take the place of persistence...
Persistence and determination alone are omnipotent."*
Calvin Coolidge

Dick Kaplan's turning point is one that taught him one of the values most fundamental to his later rise to success. While he was in grade school, Dick had something of a troubled time of it. He was held back twice and kicked out of high school no less than three times. When he actually did achieve some kind of good result, and got the highest score on his regent's test for elementary algebra, he was simply accused of cheating and forced to take it over again. Clearly, at that point in time, his reputation and self esteem weren't so great. In fact, the only thing that kept Dick going through these struggles was a distant memory of a family gathering at which his uncle, Dr. Elmer Milch, had turned to face him in front of the whole family and pronounced that Dick would be "the star of the family". Whenever he felt like giving up, he would remember this prophecy and renew his determination to fulfill it.

Despite his troublesome early days, Dick did manage to get into Monroe Community College, and he studied there for a short while before transferring to the University of Buffalo. However, one day he received some shattering news. Back home his 29 year old brother, who helped their father run the family carpeting business, had died after a long bout with cancer. Dick's father and mother were devastated and began to withdraw into themselves, ignoring the family business. Within just a short amount of time the business was in serious trouble, and desperate to help out his family, Dick quit the University of Buffalo in order to return home and tend to matters personally. Though he had worked hard to get into college and had made it despite the naysaying of many others, Dick nevertheless felt obligated to return and help his ailing parents and their business. As a result, his academic career was cut short.

When he got home, Dick found that the situation was actually somewhat more dire than he had originally imagined. His father had often sunk his own money into the company to take care of expenses as they arose and to keep the customers happy. His father therefore had little savings to take care of things when the company suddenly found itself in debt after the death of Dick's brother.

Knowing he would need a bank loan to save the family business, Dick went to their bank to borrow money and rebuild the business. There, he met with a loan officer who, without even knowing it, taught him a very important lesson. "There's no way I can loan you this money with the business in the state it's in," the lender told Dick. For a moment, it seemed as if his hopes were crushed. But then the lender followed up with something unexpected. "However," he went on, "I'm going to lend you the money because I know your father. If you're anything like him, I know I'm not going to regret it."

Dick thought of his father's commitment to customer satisfaction, and he now saw that both this and his father's reputation were the critical instruments for getting the business back on its feet. Reputation, he learned, was everything in business.

Having received the loan on the good faith of the lender, Dick worked at his father's business and helped to turn things around. Drawing on the support of the company's long-standing customer base, Dick continued to realize the positive impression that his father's reputation had had upon these people and vowed to live up to it.

Apart from the lessons he learned about reputation, however, there were many other methods that Dick undertook to make himself a more effective businessman. To begin with, he took to heart the advice given by a successful businessman he knew by the name of Harry Mangurian Jr., whose philosophy was that if you wanted to become a truly successful businessman, you needed to learn to promote your products and to get your name out there rather than waiting for others to come in the door. Dick integrated this into his approach at running the family business, and as a result he was quickly able to pay back the loan and get the business back in the black again. Having done so, he helped his father into retirement and took over most matters on his own.

Equally influential was the advice of his friend Chuck Mills, who told Dick: **"If you're going to work, do something with a huge potential."** Though others had seen the carpet business as something limited, Dick knew otherwise. Eventually, Dick saw an opportunity to seize on the true potential of the industry, and founded a company called the Maxin Group. The Maxin Group was a collection of Dick's businesses that were each involved in different aspects of the carpet industry, such that the whole formed an entirely cohesive combine. Dick did very well for himself by starting this group which eventually became a public company on the New York Stock Exchange.

After a time, Dick left the company thinking he was retired from a business career, and he did some ventures such as writing a book and running for US Congress - which he lost. Dick was eventually asked by some investors in the company Pictometry to come in and turn their operations around. Much like his taking over the family carpet business, and his experience with the Maxin Group, this also proved to be an incredibly successful venture for Dick.

Having achieved substantial success for himself, Dick continues to find ways to give back to the community. At present, he is working on an updated edition of his book called "Time for Caring". When asked to indicate the core principle of the belief system that has brought him so far, Dick doesn't run short on wisdom:

> **"In each life there is a time to give and a time to receive...Only when there is a true joy in giving and dignity in receiving can human spirits be uplifted and the C.A.R.I.N.G. cycle be completed."**

Coming from someone who made great changes in his own life and ultimately arrived at such success, the words have a ring of truth that is hard to come by.

Dennis Kessler

Co-owner Kessler Restaurants, Inc. & Executive Professor of Entrepreneurship at University of Rochester

"History has demonstrated that the most notable winners usually encounter heart breaking obstacles before they triumphed. They won because they refused to become discouraged by their defeats."
BC Forbes

Sometimes, the turning point that shapes a person's life and success can't actually be pinned down to a single influential moment. At times, turning points take other forms, such as a philosophy that the person holds throughout their life, or perhaps a certain figure who provides them with useful and helpful guidance. In the case of Dennis Kessler, the defining element in his life is not so much any single thing that happened to him, but rather the influence of his father.

From an early age, Dennis' father exercised a positive influence over his work ethic. He himself was a successful business owner who took only one

day off a month, and who encouraged Dennis to find a job at a very young age. Dennis was only 12 when he became a newspaper boy for the New York Post. He made a 2 cent profit on sales, the first money he ever earned by his own effort. Even to this day, he doesn't speak down at or belittle the position; rather, he exalts it for all the practical skills it taught him: the principles of customer service, how to keep books and financial records, how to keep track of bills and even how to fold newspapers in such a way as to streamline his operation and cut down on wasted time. Inspired by his early success at this job, he went on to look for opportunities wherever he could find them: shoveling snow for neighbors and even beginning a coin collection that he would later sell for $20,000.

Not all of Dennis' early years were so idyllic, though. In today's world, Dennis would have probably been diagnosed with Attention Deficit Disorder, but in the time he grew up in, that disability was unheard of and he was simply thought of as "stupid" for his inability to stay focused in long classes at school. By the time he was in high school, Dennis was placed in a classroom full of kids who were considered to have little to no future. Nevertheless, he doesn't consider that any of this ultimately held him back. Rather, it taught him that if he wanted something, he had to work hard for it, and work hard he did to overcome the challenge of his disability and succeed.

He graduated in 1966, whereupon he felt relieved to have exited the world of academia and was eager to join the workforce. He sent an application to Charles Pfizer and Co, Inc. to work as a stock clerk, and was shocked when he received a rejection letter from them; so shocked that he preserved the letter and for many years it hung on his wall as motivation, although for a time, Dennis wasn't quite sure what he should be motivated towards. Searching for direction after high school, Dennis attended a job fair hoping to find employment. There, a government worker reviewed Dennis' records and encouraged him to continue his education, assuring him that not only did he have the talent, but that he would find the atmosphere of college a lot more accommodating to individualistic learning styles than high school was.

Realizing a worthwhile job wasn't just going to be handed to him, Dennis began to consider college and his father's advice:

"If you want it, you have to earn it!"

Thus inspired, Dennis went on to City University of New York and in 1970, received a degree in sociology. Thereafter, he sought employment as a New York City cab driver, but failed the written exam that was required to secure the job. Luckily, his father was once again prepared to step in and bolster and guide the young Dennis, more or less forcing him to take the test again. Of course, he passed the second time.

Although at first his ambition was to join the workforce and escape from academia, Dennis found his impressions changing the more time he spent in a cab getting to know people. He soon felt the calling to return to school and earned his masters degree in Sociology. Not content to stop there, he went on to apply to NYU to get into their PhD program and was accepted. Dennis continued to sail forth in his academic career, having developed a newfound love for learning and the opportunities that it opened up, when he hit something of a brick wall. When it came time for him to complete graduate school, he had to turn in a dissertation. His dissertation advisor, however, was someone that Dennis described as an "extremely hostile person," an ex-convict whose political and economic views clashed mightily with Dennis' own. Rather than render an objective view of the quality of Dennis' dissertation, the advisor kept him on the ropes for quite a long time. Knowing that his graduation would be held up indefinitely by this person, Dennis recalled another critical piece of advice from his father:

"Life is always full of hurdles... so move the hurdles!"

Dennis left NYU, having nearly met all the requirements for a degree, and then he went on to law school at Yale and received his degree there.

However, Dennis was never to take the bar and never to practice law. Soon after he graduated, his brother Larry (whose own story is detailed elsewhere in this book) approached him with a solid business plan that proved to be profitable for the both of them. Drawing on the skills that he had learned from all his years in school, Dennis helped his brother in the buying and running of several restaurant franchises.

Though the two of them would go on to meet with great success, it didn't happen overnight. There was a serious downturn in the economy and interest rates skyrocketed to 17%. The time came when they owed $100,000 to the state of New York in sales tax, and they had already spent that money on other things. It was simply no longer there to pay the bills. Desperate, Dennis and Larry borrowed the money from their father and paid it back over the next five years.

They continued to slowly build their business, a piece at a time, into the solid and successful enterprise that it's become today. It was the influence of his father that helped Dennis steer clear of disaster. Dennis and Larry tried to adhere to the philosophy of their father that **there are no "home runs" in business, and you have to build up your reputation and success slowly, a solid piece at a time**.

Though his rise to success has met with several changes of course, setbacks and outright stumbles along the way, Dennis has always held fast to his father's beliefs, including one of the most important ones:

"Don't want any business problems? Go deliver the mail."

Knowing that he could simply give up and take an easier line of work was all it really took to keep Dennis motivated. He knew that obstacles were par for the course from the moment he set out, and what's more, he knew that he had the ability to meet and overcome them.

Not surprisingly, Dennis continues to challenge himself to this day. He gives back to the community by teaching at the University of Rochester's Simon School of Business, where he holds an endowed chair in entrepreneurship. Not bad for someone who started out in a classroom full of criminals. Of course, as Dennis is always the first to acknowledge, he's had a little help along the way.

Turning Points

<u>Larry Kessler</u>

Co-owner Kessler Restaurants, Inc.

*"If no one ever took risks, Michelangelo would have painted
the Sistine floor."*
Neil Simon

Larry Kessler's turning point is one that he describes as a
"2x4 experience". What he means by that is an experience
that, in no uncertain terms, hit him square between the eyes
and shocked him out of something of a trance state in which
he'd been living his life up to that point.

*In 1965, Larry was attending law school at St.
John's University, because at that time the best
careers for Jewish students were either medicine or
law. Thinking no more of it, or perhaps not
thinking of it at all, Larry followed along the path
that had been set out for him until the point that he
was dismissed from law school for failing an
elective course. At the time, St. John's had a
stricter requirement for all Jewish students and
failure in even an elective course resulted in an
immediate dismissal. The blow was one that went
unforeseen by Larry and totally took him off guard.
Here he was, at the age when most other people*

103

were just beginning their careers, and he had just flunked out of law school and had no idea what he was going to do with himself.

Soon after he flunked out of school, Larry received some helpful advice from his father that he ended up taking to heart. "Larry," his father said to him:

"How you make your bed is how you sleep in it."

Though it was something of a catastrophe at the time, today Larry views it as the turning point in his life. Considering the success he's made of himself since then, this can hardly be seen as a bad thing. But let's not get too far ahead of ourselves.

Understanding that his father meant that you're the master of your own destiny, Larry went out in search of work. Finding a position in sales, Larry rose to the top very quickly. After only a short time, he had achieved the highest level of sales in his firm, working as a pharmaceutical sales representative. Feeling that he had exhausted his potential in that market and wanting to diversify his experience, Larry branched out and took a job as a stockbroker. This was a risky maneuver, but it proved to be a wildly successful one. He became the first Jewish vice president in his firm while still in his 20's. In the 1970's, only a handful of years after he had experienced what he had thought of as a major defeat, he was with yet another top company and found himself being appointed their senior vice president.

In everyone's eyes, Larry had reached the heights of success. And yet, somewhere inside him, the desire for something more was brewing. His work experiences had shown him that he had excellent top-tier potential in both sales and leadership. These were talents that he didn't want to go to waste. He considered his background and thought of Wolf's, the successful delicatessen that his father had been running in New York for quite some time. Though the jump seemed logical from his perspective, it must have come as a big shock to everyone else when he announced that he was leaving his successful senior vice president position to work at a Burger King. Larry sought his father's advice, something he always did throughout his career. He again received a comforting affirmation of his abilities when his father told him **"it's only a job, seek your star"**.

To be more specific, he intended to purchase a Burger King franchise in upstate New York. Despite this shift being viewed with skepticism at best, or outright derision at worst from most people he knew, Larry ended up making the jump at the age of 31, with a three year old daughter to support.

Like the other ventures Larry had set out on, his Burger King franchise seemed to turn to gold at his very touch. But however easy it seemed to those on the outside, Larry put in countless hours seven days a week, doing everything from cleaning the bathrooms to serving guests. Before long, he had three successful restaurants under his command, and along with his brother Dennis (also profiled in this book), developed and purchased quite a few more. In time, he was approached by a group of investment bankers, who would give Larry what would shape up to be his second turning point.

The investment bankers had a large group of restaurant franchises that they wanted him to take over, based on his success with the Burger Kings he already owned. At first Larry turned them down outright, preferring to concentrate on his own plans. But when they kept approaching him time after time, he eventually signed a confidentiality agreement in order to get more information. When he did, Larry said he became even more adamant about turning them down. The restaurants in question were all Friendly's, a full-service chain. Considering the purchase incompatible with his fast food experience, Larry expressed his reluctance to the sellers. In the end, however, their continued persistence made him take another look. He went to visit the franchises in question and as he says "there was low hanging fruit". In other words, there was some key potential to each one that could be capitalized on by an owner who had the right mentality: an owner's mentality rather than a corporate mentality. Deciding that the opportunity was just too great, Larry made the purchase.

In no time at all, his unique approach to business and his good work ethic had turned the franchises around, and they became some of the most profitable Friendly's in the country. Although the Friendly's brand has changed hands several times since then, Larry says that he's held fast, and to this date he's so well-respected that he's always approached by the corporate headquarters when they have decisions to make. He and his brother are the largest and most profitable franchise holders in the entire corporation.

When asked what lesson he took away from the experience, Larry has this to say:

"The key to good negotiation is not wanting it so badly."

His reluctance to purchase initially had caused the sellers to return to him time and time again, each time with a more favorable offer. He eventually found out that the group was having financial difficulties and he could have virtually named his own price. Since then, this detached "take it as it comes" approach to negotiation has served him well.

Ever since Larry "woke up" thanks to his St. John's experience and discovered the true heights of his professional potential, he's showed no signs at all of stopping. Outside of work, he maintains an active lifestyle with his involvement with the RRDC, a racing club for sports car enthusiasts that ranks among the top 1% of drivers in the amateur racing community. Despite being sixty-five years old, he says he just doesn't understand the retirement personality, indicating a love of his work that is enviable. He says:

"If you like what you do, you never have to work a day in your life".

Coming from someone who knows what it's like to be left with nothing, Larry is evidence that it's never too late for a single turning point to turn one's life completely around.

Turning Points

Earl Krakower

Realtor Coldwell Banker Prime Properties

"We can achieve anything we want to achieve, but first we must have the courage to believe we can achieve it."
Tony Gordon

Having spent most of his adult life in Rochester, NY in a successful career as a Professor of Chemistry at RIT, Earl Krakower is, with his wife Esther, one of the most successful and foremost realtors in the region. What makes his story so interesting, though, is that he entered the real estate market at the age of 57.

Earl says he had his turning point in an instant, one morning back in 1996. Here's how he describes it:

"I knew mentally that as good as everything was, and although I could have stayed at RIT for the rest of my life, I knew that a change may be welcome.

> **It was just something instinctive in my body that told me that even though I had a stable and prosperous position for 30 years, it might be fun to have a change away from the natural progression."**
>
> **And so, instead of continuing on that natural progression, Earl left Rochester Institute of Technology for a new career. It was his desire for a challenge, and his respect and admiration for the many entrepreneurial risks that his wife had taken over the years (risks that had paid off) that prompted him to go to work for her.**

Earl and Esther both grew up in Montreal, Canada. Earl pursued his undergraduate degree at McGill University in Montreal, and in 1960 moved to Vancouver, British Columbia to earn his PhD at the University of British Columbia at the age of 23. He says he was on the verge of accepting a job offer there, an offer that had been made to him a mere day after he received his doctorate, when a last minute phone call at 7:00 AM from the Dean of Science at RIT changed everything. A gut instinct that he should accept the position, as well as the convenient fact that he'd be moving closer to family on the East Coast, prompted Earl to accept the offer and make the move to Rochester.

Though he initially only intended to stay with RIT for five to ten years, his work there was successful enough to win him a tenured position that he held for thirty years. When he walked away from his secure and prosperous position to join a market in which he had no practical experience, Earl was head of his department, and had the opportunity to become a dean at another school.

Earl describes his turning point as more of a "natural evolution" in his family life rather than something motivated entirely by professional concerns. When he and Esther first moved to Rochester in September of 1966 and were looking for their first home, Esther realized that she had a talent for real estate and decided to move on it. As Earl's career as a professor at RIT developed, so too did Esther's business. And over time, she moved from a standard self-employed realtor to the Broker/Owner of Coldwell Banker.

From his work at RIT, Earl knew he had a talent for recruiting faculty members who became excellent employees for the university. He felt that his success there had some commonality with Esther's brokerage business: she recruited people to sell houses, very often from the same places that Earl found his recruits.

It was an incredible risk to be sure, but as Earl himself put it, he felt he had accomplished everything he could at RIT, and so he felt no guilt in taking his retirement. He mentions fondly that the faculty there were very supportive of his decision and he couldn't have been more delighted with the transition, even when he experienced a moment that would be horrifying to most individuals:

"At RIT, I was a tenured professor with a guaranteed salary and absolutely no stress if I didn't want the stress. Here, I woke up unemployed... and I absolutely welcomed the challenge."

His willingness, even longing, to take risks and profit from them is one of the three key things to which Earl attributes his success.

The second is that he's a very goal-oriented person. When he first went to work for the university as an assistant professor, Earl says he had certain ideas in mind about what he wanted to achieve, and he always set concrete goals. By sticking to them, he found that he received his tenure a full two years before he was scheduled to. Similarly, when he first entered the real estate market, **he set himself annual volume goals and never failed to meet them.**

The third, and perhaps the most important, is that he had a huge number of contacts in the community, not only from his work at RIT, but also from community work. Coming into the real estate business, he knew that **exercising a large sphere of influence is critical to success**, and so he has always been careful to maintain these contacts and call upon them when needed.

Not surprisingly, Earl says he has had no second thoughts about his change of career. While his position at the university was very secure, he says it was also very challenging. He compared this degree of challenge with his wife's entrepreneurial risk-taking and realized that in the 44 years married to one another, all the risks they had ever taken together had paid off. And so, he came to the game with all the optimism he needed to get him through trying times. As far as Earl is concerned, the biggest success story is when two people who are married to one another can work together for such a long period of time.

Now at age 69 when asked whether or not he plans to retire, Earl offers in one statement the final word on just how he's managed not just one, but two amazingly successful careers over the course of his life:

"I'll probably keep doing this until the day I die," he says. "I just enjoy the challenge that much."

Giovanni LiDestri

President of LiDestri Foods, Inc.

"You miss 100% of the shots you never take."
Wayne Gretzky

Giovanni LiDestri's success is one that stems from tradition. A tradition rooted in old fashioned values like devotion to one's industry, personal loyalty, the desire to succeed and be useful, as well as a solid family base that got him off to the right start. In many ways, his success story is one with all the trappings of the archetypal immigrant success story, so, it rings true and hits close to home. It would be Giovanni's devotion to these classical values and traditions, as well as an excellent sense for business, that would take him to heights of success that even he never quite dreamed of.

Giovanni first came to the United States from Italy at the age of fourteen. He was brought to the country by his mother and father, with his brother and two sisters. Whereas life in Italy had been one of relative comfort in the middle class, things were

113

different here in America. Here, the six of them lived in a crowded three room apartment where attitudes were much more liberal, allowing Giovanni's mother to take a job outside the home for the first time ever.

Giovanni's parents and family had always believed in the value of hard work and they wasted no time getting down to it. Despite several disadvantages, such as the fact that Giovanni himself couldn't speak English, everyone went to work almost immediately, with Giovanni washing bottles at the Ragu Packing Company where his brother also worked. After being in the country only nine months and saving all their money, his family was able to buy their first home. This event would help to shape Giovanni's outlook. Though he had grown up with a sense of family duty and similar values, here for the first time he really saw the potential tangible value of hard work paying off, in the form of the house that they purchased.

From the beginning, Giovanni was an exceptional study. He graduated from high school in only three years instead of four and quickly went on to college. However, his traditional hands-on type of personality left him wanting to pursue more practical work than academia would provide him. As such, despite his good grades, he dropped out of college to go to work full time at the age of 21.

The job that Giovanni took was one that would actually shape the course of his career forever. Much like the old traditionalists who practiced the value of company loyalty, he has stayed in the same base industry for the majority of his career. It all started when Ralph Cantisano, president of Ragu Packing Company (which started the Ragu line of pasta sauce), asked him if he wouldn't like to change his long-held part time position at the company into a permanent position. Giovanni accepted the offer eagerly and went to work.

It was here, in his first ever full time job, that Giovanni was able to demonstrate the real practical value of his work ethic and drive to succeed. Giovanni would perform basically every job that the company had to offer, from filing paperwork to driving a forklift and everything in between. Out of his pure desire to make himself useful and do hard, meaningful work, Giovanni learned how to work in just about every department in the entire company. He became famous for a certain catchphrase that he used to say while working there, which bears repeating here because it's really a very succinct summation of Giovanni's entire outlook on life. The very minute that one job was finished, he could be heard to remark:

"OK. Who needs me to do anything?"

No matter what the job was, Giovanni was always willing to do it, and this attitude would quickly come to pay off. In 1969, just one year after he started working there full time, the company was sold to new owners. When the Cantisano family sold Ragu to Chesebrough-Ponds (now Unilever), they granted the employees a share of the proceeds, and Giovanni was awarded a $48,000 dollar bonus - at the time an enormous sum to him - as thanks for a job well done.

Much as his parents before him had used their work ethic to build a new life for themselves, Giovanni did the same: he put $10,000 of that $48,000 down on a new house.

Giovanni's reputation as a "mover and shaker" at Ragu paid off, when Ralph Cantisano later called Giovanni to run a cheese manufacturing company that Ralph had subsequently purchased. Ralph had seen an intriguing entrepreneurial opportunity in the cheese factory, but quickly found that the industry was rife with all kinds of technical problems particular to the making of cheese, like the problem of waste water disposal. Ralph was looking for someone dependable who could help them turn the business around. That's when he offered the job to Giovanni. At the time he received this offer to work with Ralph again, Giovanni didn't know that the cheese company wasn't doing so well. But he was eager to have the opportunity to work with Ralph again and loved the promise of a new challenge. Giovanni became General Manager of the cheese company and led it to modest success in a fairly short period of time, but knew there wasn't much more he could do to grow it.

Despite his success there, Giovanni once again felt that he could be applying his talents in a more profound way, so he approached Ralph and found that Ralph was experiencing similar feelings. Reminiscing over the good times that they'd had working together at Ragu Packing Company, the two of them decided to return to their roots and get back into the pasta sauce business. Ralph would put up the money for the equipment and Giovanni would manage the business - his dedication to getting the job done and his experience as a successful manager, both being valuable assets.

When they began their new business, Cantisano Foods, they initially focused on the food service rather than the retail side of things. Before long, their gamble had paid off once again. Giovanni eventually bought the company from Ralph, and today Giovanni's company makes tomato-based products for the retail market as well, selling their proprietary brands Francesco-Rinaldi Pasta Sauces and Sante Fe Salsa, in addition to making sauces for many other well-known companies such as Heinz, Frito-Lay, Nestle and Newman's Own, as well as store brands like Wegmans. Giovanni's business continues to grow each and every year, overcoming challenges along the way for the sheer joy of doing successful business.

Giovanni's success, in a way, almost seemed inevitable. While he certainly had to work hard to get to where he is today, his devotion to the value of hard work is so strong that it seems almost in-born.

Indeed, it seems to be this devotion more than anything else that has brought him to where he stands today as one of the most successful entrepreneurs of his generation. It was a dream that first began to materialize with that house purchased by his parents nine months after arriving in America; a dream born of hard work, loyalty and perseverance.

Turning Points

<u>Dan Meyers</u>

President of the Al Sigl Center

"It is in giving that we receive."
St. Francis of Assisi

In April 1971, Dan Meyers faced the single most defining moment of his life. But like so many involved in a career of service, it wouldn't be only his life that was affected by this defining moment, but the lives of thousands of people in and around the Rochester community. It all started when Dan took a college job working as the night janitor for the Association for the Blind and Visually Impaired (ABVI). He had intended it only to be a temporary assignment, but as the date of his graduation approached, he was offered a permanent position at the Association, as their Director of Recreation and Volunteers. Dan was conflicted about which path to choose. On the one hand, it was a rather good start in the service career; but on the other hand, he had already made plans for himself for a cross-country road trip after graduation, to gain valuable "life experience".

Dan turned down the job offer because he felt that his road trip was simply too important an experience, and that it was something he wouldn't

be able to do at any other time in his life. However, in what must have seemed like a flash of destiny, circumstances aligned to prevent Dan from taking that trip. The car he had planned to use suddenly broke down for seemingly no reason and Dan was without the money needed to repair it. He took it as a sign and decided to make the best of his situation. He returned to ABVI and asked them if their job offer still stood. It did, he accepted it, and that marked the beginning of a life dedicated to service.

Dan's history had done much to prepare him for such a life. He had always been raised to understand the importance of giving back to the community, and had excellent role models to guide him. His father, who worked for Kodak his entire career, often served as chairman on various charitable committees. In addition, his mother would bring him along on door to door solicitations for the Mother's March of Dimes against Polio. His school days were also formative, in that he went away to a Catholic high school where for four years he was required to give weekly speeches in front of the whole class. This granted him an excellent ability to communicate and connect with others. The combination of this ability to connect with the desire to improve the lives of those around him, made Dan a good fit for the role he took on at the ABVI.

Dan's major contribution at ABVI was to collaborate on a national demonstration project, the goal of which was to help integrate older people with vision problems into active community programs for seniors. As a result of his work there, he was invited to a prestigious White House Conference on Aging. He came away from that experience convinced there were great opportunities in the not-for-profit sector and enormous challenges for people with disabilities and special needs. His first position would begin a chain reaction of successful leadership positions in not-for-profit organizations, eliminating challenges and opening opportunities.

Dan eventually moved on to start the Retired Senior Volunteer Program at Lifespan, a non for profit organization, where he helped create new opportunities for active seniors. He played the part of Santa Claus for an audience of retirees at the George Eastman House, unaware that it was dress rehearsal for a position they would offer him when he became their first Director of Development.

Within a year, he had become the acting director. He considers this another major turning point in his career because it was a "sink or swim" scenario. He had no real experience as a director but knew that he had to succeed if he and the museum were to survive and grow. It was a tough assignment, but in the end he saw it through before moving on to work with the Rochester Philharmonic Orchestra, where he directed a major fundraising campaign.

When he was 39, Dan became the first Executive Director at the Al Sigl Center. Coincidently, the Center was also the place he chose to do his volunteering from the time he graduated. So now he found himself being paid to be in the place where his heart had led him. It has been an all encompassing role, and it has continually presented new challenges and opportunities for achieving more together.

After 20 years at Al Sigl Center, Dan has this to say on the meaning of his entire career:

> **"If you tie yourself to causes that you believe in with all your heart, as I have been fortunate to do in my professional life and in my volunteer life, you always find it within yourself to give what you have and ask for whatever else is needed."**

This lesson applies not only to charity, but to those in all areas of business. The more passionately devoted one is to one's work, the more likely one is to succeed because one will naturally work the hardest and be the most effective.

Of course, Dan's story doesn't stop there. In 2000, he was named Fundraising Executive of the Year by the International Association of Fundraising Professionals, that organization's highest honor. However, he doesn't dwell on this laudable achievement and use it as an excuse to rest on his laurels; instead, he has this to say:

"That was yesterday... there's much more to do."

In May of 2005, Dan spoke to the graduating class at Nazareth College, where he was also being awarded an honorary degree. Realizing the need for a message that was both short and powerful, Dan spoke about what he knew best and imparted to them the message that **"when one serves, good things happen"**.

Tirelessly dedicated to his passions, Dan stands as a shining example of what is possible when one commits one's self to one's work whole-heartedly and without reservation.

Mike Nuccitelli

CEO and President of Parlec, Inc

"To exist is to change, to change is to mature,
to mature is to go on creating oneself endlessly."
Henri Louis Bergson

Getting to the core of Mike Nuccitelli was as simple as
mentioning the high school Mike graduated from in 1980,
Aquinas Institute. If it hadn't been for his father, the
"Aquinas Connection" would not be there. Growing up in the
Jay Street, Orchard Street area in Rochester NY in the
1940s-1950s, going to Aquinas was a dream – one which
came true when he approached the school and they invited
him to attend. Of course, he could not pay the tuition, but
they "worked it out" and his father graduated in 1955. Given
Mike's background and upbringing, it can truly be said of him
that he's no stranger to hard work. Since the age of five,
he's been working in some capacity or another; it was this
lifetime of experience working around other people, viewing
their individual strengths and weaknesses, and seeing what
business practices worked and which didn't that added up to

become the "turning point" that has enabled him to go on to become the great success that he is today.

Born in Rochester, New York in 1962, Mike first began his career in his father's shop sweeping floors and then worked his way up to selling hot dogs, hamburgers and lemonade to workers putting in the new city sewer system at the age of seven. He began selling apples at the age of eight, cutting lawns and performing various other odd jobs from ages nine to eleven. But it was when he turned thirteen that he was given his first "real" job, an experience that would forever change him. He was employed by his father to come and work at Nationwide Tool & Die on Exchange Street in Rochester. In this first job Mike was paid $2.50 an hour to wash the windows, a figure that seemed astronomical to him at the time.

He still recalls the very first day working for pay in his father's shop. Mike spent several hours procuring all his cleaning supplies and setting up all the necessary buckets and ladders. He finally got to work and by the time he had washed only one window, he heard a bell. He was shocked when he realized that it was the bell signaling the morning coffee break for the shop's employees. The older workers called for Mike to come along with them, but he seemed confused at first, wondering how it was that he was expected to take a break when he had only washed one window so far! His dedication was noticed by his co-workers and won him immediate respect.

What really made this experience working in his father's shop such a turning point, however, is that Mike was able for the first time to see all kinds of different personalities at work, and perceive how they each helped to contribute to the overall success of the company.

From bottom to top, Mike realized that everyone had something to contribute, and that even the so-called "problem employees" had the ability to contribute if they were only put in positions where they could excel. This really helped to shape the managerial strategies that define Mike's approach to business and his almost uncanny knack for turning seemingly negative situations into wild successes. As he puts it:

"It is what it is."

A simple quote, but a very revealing one as Mike goes on to explain. He has always been able to look at mistakes and see the underlying value, the attempt at success that might have fallen just a little short. As he tells his employees, he always thinks it better to strive for a 7 to 10 win/loss record, than a 3 to 3. Because he is able to see the value in any situation and take advantage of it, he is never afraid to take risks and this, he says, has made all the difference.

There are several instances throughout Mike's life where his risk-taking personality has won the day. The first occurrence was when he was preparing to enter college. Mike was a hockey player at the time and found himself with an offer to play for the Canadian Junior A team, as well as an offer to play for the University of Dayton on a full scholarship. On the other hand, he had the opportunity with no guarantees at all to go to Clarkson University, a school renowned for their engineering program, which is what Mike had always wanted to major in. In the end he opted for Clarkson, and although he was cut from the varsity hockey team and relegated to playing junior varsity, he would go on to graduate with honors.

From there, Mike had no immediate plans to go to work for his father's business, but at his uncle's behest he was eventually swayed. Although he would have to turn down two prestigious offers from GE in Syracuse and Texas Instruments in Dallas and accept a 33% cut in salary, Mike stayed with his father's company, certain that there was a place there for him with his new knowledge of sales and engineering, and that he could turn the already very successful company into something more than it was. This was another gamble, of course, but in the end it did pay off. Within three years of graduating from college, at age 26, Mike had been named President of the company and within five years, he had quadrupled their profits.

This resounding success was the result of yet another risky maneuver that Mike embarked upon. When he first joined his father's company, their primary client was Xerox, providing what Mike estimated was at least 95% of all the company's profits. Though most people were content with this situation that had admittedly been working quite well for many years, Mike became concerned that if anything were to ever happen to Xerox, their own company wouldn't be able to stay afloat. Of course, in the late 80s, Xerox did suffer some major setbacks. Luckily, in the meantime Mike had spent several years on the road, going across the country in an attempt to gain new contracts. His skills gained observing different types of people and recognizing their value had won him quite a few friends at Chrysler Corporation, thanks in large part to Mike's spending a lot of personal time with them, joining them on outings to their favorite bars and restaurants and in general winning their trust. When the time came for Chrysler to look for a new supplier, the contract went to the most obvious choice, Mike. It was this multi-million dollar contract that Mike sought out that not only kept the company afloat throughout the collapse of Xerox, but also allowed it to prosper.

Mike has gone on to achieve one success after another throughout his career, from buying into the hugely successful Parlec, Inc. in 1990 with his partner, Ron Ricotta, and eventually selling his father's company in 1999. He still attributes all of his victories to those same primary factors: the understanding of people that a life in the workplace afforded him, the ability to see a good thing in the midst of a bad situation, and the willingness to take chances. When asked for advice he might give to others, Mike indicates that this formula for success is not unique to him:

"Most people have an opportunity to change their life. It's a matter of whether or not they recognize it and then take advantage of that opportunity... that's my core belief."

Turning Points

Ron Ricotta

CEO of Century Mold

*"Destiny is not a matter of chance, it is a matter of choice;
it is not a thing to be waited for, it is a thing to be achieved."*
William Jennings Bryan

Ron Ricotta's turning point ought to be one that many of us can easily identify with. As a child, he had worked the same odd jobs as his friends, with the exception that he did two or three times as many of them, giving up the opportunity to play in order to focus on his work. His work ethic was astonishing, and no one ever doubted that he would put in the effort that was required to secure a good job and make an excellent living at it. Ron, however, wanted something more than that. More than just a lucrative job, more even than just a partnership in a profitable firm, Ron wanted independence and freedom. He wanted to own his own business so that he could work for himself, set his own terms, and keep the entirety of the fruits of his labor. When Ron was 36 he would see his dream come true; it was the major turning point in his life. To fully understand the context of that changeover and what it meant to Ron, we must go back a little and start at the beginning.

When Ron left college, he went straight into accounting in the hopes of making the most of his degree and education. He made a pretty good living, but there was something missing. Ron realized a crucial difference between working for someone else and working for himself; namely that in one instance, one's capacity to earn was limited, while in the other, it was dependent entirely on how much work one put in. Determined to fall into the latter category, Ron resolved that by the time he was thirty, he would become a partner in his accounting firm, effectively able to control his own destiny.

Ron did eventually meet his goal and became partner at his accounting firm, as he had expected to. However, Ron always had it in the back of his mind that this was only a momentary stop on the road; he might be in a better position, but he still hadn't reached his ultimate goal of working for himself in a company of his own.

Ron worked in the accounting firm for a total of thirteen years before he decided it was time for a drastic change and submitted his resignation. Throwing himself into the void to either sink or swim is what he describes as his turning point, the point when he knew that either his principles would pay off and he would be a success, or he would be mistaken about his own abilities and become a failure, left with nothing. Of course, Ron had already achieved a great deal of success in becoming a partner, so it's no surprise that his dedication to hard work and steadfast advancement paid off once more.

During Ron's stint as a public accountant, he spent much of his time working with manufacturing companies. As a result of that experience, he felt that this would be the best avenue he could go down after leaving the firm.

He went to work for a company called Nationwide, a privately held firm owned by the Nuccitelli family, and became partner. He was asked to help save an ailing sister company called Parlec and help turn it around. He worked with Mike Nuccitelli, who handled the sales and engineering side of the equation, while Ron handled the operations and finance side. Before long their efforts started to see results, thanks to a strategy they implemented of rearranging the work force to have certain people work in the areas they were best suited for. The combined companies went from a 16 million dollar business to a 55 million dollar business in only six years.

It was a success as they had been hoping for, but Ron wasn't finished yet. Fresh from his successful turnaround of the company, the Nuccitelli family was approached with an offer to sell Nationwide, and they accepted it. Ron stayed on for two years as president, working under the new owner. However, he realized that **once you have a taste for your own business, it is hard to work for someone else, and there's no going back.**

So Ron went back to Parlec to work with Mike, but unfortunately this was just before September 11th. The industry again went through a hard time, and the company was in need of saving once more. After two years of tough times, they managed to bring the company back once more.

Thus emboldened by his success, Ron and Mike would go on to purchase another manufacturing company, this one called Century Mold. It was essentially in the same industry as Nationwide, only it was involved in plastics rather than metals. Here, Ron's dedication, work ethic, and doing things the right way won him his most profound success ever. While Century Mold was originally a 27 million dollar business when he walked into it, Ron turned it into an 85 million dollar business in only 5 years.

Ever since then Ron has continued to work as his own boss, setting his own terms and constantly pushing forward, never satisfied to let things stay as they are. Though he's now in his fifties and certainly has the capital that would let him retire comfortably, he doesn't even consider it an option. For him, it's not just about the money, but rather the thrill that he gets from committing to his own decisions and then seeing them pan out successfully. Ron describes that the biggest mistake he has made in business is not following his own gut instincts.

> **"I would say when something feels a little uncomfortable and I get talked into it, those have been my biggest mistakes."**

When things run smoothly as a result of his organization, he says, that's the greatest high that he can imagine. That's one of the major appeals in working for himself, and not something that he's ready to abandon.

When asked about the secret of his success, Ron is very straightforward. He says simply that he believes in hard work and doing the right thing. He makes quality products because those are the kind of products that he himself would want to buy, and the commitment to quality has paid off massively. To put it in his own words:

"When you have to make a decision, just do the right thing."

Simple advice, perhaps, but sometimes the simplest approach reaps the biggest rewards. It certainly has for Ron Ricotta.

<u>Richard Sands</u>

Chairman Constellation Brands

"The purpose of this life and all its experiences is not to make ourselves what we think we should be. It is to unfold who we already are."
Gary Zukav from Seat of the Soul

Richard Sands' success has always been inextricably intertwined with his environment and the people that he has around him. Understanding has always been his primary goal, and he has certainly demonstrated a knack for it. Richard has the unique capacity to look at both a set of numbers and a group of people, and fully understand the intricacies and inner-workings of both. He is equally capable of mathematically analyzing a situation and producing a highly accurate statistical modeling analysis, as he is putting people first and figuring out what drives them and how best to do business with them. It's this devotion to understanding more than anything that has made him a success in business.

Richard grew up in the 1960's and was most definitely a product of that generation's influences. He held liberal values and whether they were systems of numbers or people, was more interested in the unspoken dynamics of systems than he was in concrete matters like dollars and cents; in other words, he was a self-described hippie. He went to the University of California in Berkeley, but dropped out of school at the age of 21 because he had no particular idea what it was that he wanted to do. Like many of today's successful business owners, he comes from a family background rooted in the area: both his grandfather Mack and his father Marvin had worked in the family business and achieved a good deal of success there. Despite that, however, they were sympathetic to the idiosyncrasies of the new generation, and Richard never felt any particular obligation to enter into the family business. As such, he resisted it for a while.

Continuing to pursue his education, Richard had two major influences acting upon him. He recalled that, while driving him to religious school on Saturday mornings, his father would teach him mathematics - and algebra in particular. This approach had allowed him a unique understanding of mathematics and numbers, an understanding that seemed to elude his classmates who were more interested in rote memorization than truly understanding the formula they were using. On the other hand, his interest in what drives people to behave the way they do was strong as well. Looking for a field where he could flex both sides of his intellectual muscle equally, he decided to get a PhD in social psychology from the University of North Carolina. That didn't come easily, though.

When Richard was writing his dissertation, he quickly realized that the scope of the work was so great that it would take him at least another year and a half to complete it. Having no desire to stay in school that long, he told his father that he was considering quitting. Knowing that leaving such a huge task unfinished would always bother his son,

Richard's father convinced him to reduce the scope of his dissertation and get his degree within a few months, and moreover that when he had finished, they could talk about Richard coming to work for him. His father spoke of the role of "social entrepreneurship", and how a dedicated entrepreneur could use his or her financial success to enact positive changes in the lives of others. Thus emboldened, he decided to join up with the family business.

The business, called Constellation Brands, is the world's largest producer of wine and spirits. Richard worked alongside his father in managing the company, drawing on the expertise that he had taken away from his college experiences to give him insights into employee behavior and desires. Before long, he was surprised to find himself thrust into the primary leadership role as his father fell ill. While his father was out, Richard continued to implement his people-oriented approach to business management and adopted the philosophy learned from his father that he calls the "hub and spokes" approach. Namely, he operates as the hub of a wheel, around which the spokes (the individual members of the management team) revolve. It takes the cooperation of the two in order to get anywhere. In addition, he used his mathematical modeling skills to make some very wise acquisitions of other companies, which helped the business to grow in dramatic and unexpected ways. In other words, as a leader, he was a resounding success.

Richard's dedication to running a business from the standpoint of understanding how things work has clearly made all the difference in his career. Since he was a young boy, he had been disinterested in the typical strategies of business and preferred to **focus on figuring out the minds of those individuals who make up the business, learning what made them tick.** This interest has given him the amazing ability to aid them in working together in a way that has brought outrageously successful results, as well as an appreciation for the quirks of life in general. To put it in Richard's own words,

> **"As much as people think they actually control their destiny and their lives, I'm not sure it's not a random walk. We don't always make our own decisions. Even when we think we are, those decisions are reactions... they lead us to a place we never would have imagined."**

This "big-picture" perspective for how humans work and interact with one another is something that only Richard could have brought to the table, and capitalizing upon it has given him a definitive edge in business.

This perspective has also helped Richard and the company to weather the many ups and downs that life has thrown at them. For example, in the early 80's, with the introduction of California-based wine coolers to the marketplace, Richard and his father looked to start their own wine cooler brand. They did so successfully, but unforeseen market forces ended up turning on them and costing them quite a lot of money. However, it was viewed by everyone involved as a valuable learning experience, something that would not have been the case in a company that was focused on the bottom line of profit over understanding and long term growth!

Like many businessmen from that generation, Richard's success in business lies soundly in his unique approach to business strategy. His dedication to his ideals is inspiring in the way he has made them work for him in practical reality, building up the business of his father and grandfather to become something that no one ever expected. As such, Richard's story is a perfect model of the success that one can achieve by adhering to the kind of ideals that the competition might be lacking.

His ideas don't stop at the office, though. Recently, he passed the CEO role to his brother Rob, which allows Richard to devote much of his time and money to charitable causes in an effort to give back to the community. Through the years, he has given an astonishing amount of money to various charities, as well as establishing his own charitable institutions, and he estimates that he presently spends nearly half of his time driving the ultimate agenda and direction of his charitable interests.   Richard founded Education Enterprises of New York in order to help learning disabled children and their parents. In this way, he not only continues the traditions that led to his own success, but ensures that his values will continue to live on in future generations.

Turning Points

Steven Sauer

President Toshiba Business Solutions

"The difference between a successful person and others is not a lack of strength, not a lack of knowledge, but rather a lack of will."
Vincent Lombardi

If work ethic could be given a name and a face, it would be that of Steven Sauer. From a very early age, Steven knew that he wanted to one day work for himself and on his own terms. He dreamed of becoming successful and considered many different ways that this could happen, including being a professional hockey player. However, he harbored no delusions about what it would take to make that happen and began saving early on. From the very beginning, he has worked tirelessly and endlessly to set himself up for the kind of success he wanted to achieve. The road, however, was not without some setbacks; or more precisely, what appeared to be setbacks that were in actuality turning points. At these crossroads, Steven would see firsthand that his dedication to hard work was what was needed to give him the leverage to get ahead of the competition.

The major turning point in reaching this realization is the regimen that he imposed upon himself in order to win his first job out of college in the management training program at Chase Manhattan Bank. Steven sought out the job because he had worked an internship with a company called Business Methods while in school, and their president informed him that the very best first job an up and coming businessman could take was that of a commercial banker. His reasoning behind that was that the position gave one a unique perspective to view the attitudes of entrepreneurs, and to observe which of their propositions eventually met with success and which fell through.

The prospect sounded great to Steven, who wanted any advantage he could get to set him on his way to the life and job of his dreams. However, he knew that securing the position with Chase would be a very competitive process. To be specific, there were 1100 applicants and only six positions open. With the odds not looking good, Steven knew that he had to leverage any advantage he could possibly have in order to set himself apart from the crowd.

In what he describes as one of the most arduous and demanding times of his life, Steven underwent an intense period to balance being the student president of the business school, his involvement in the college senate, and working part time up to 4 hours a day to help pay for his school - all which was designed to give him the kind of skills and impressive resume that would be required to take the Chase interview by storm. To prepare for the interview, he recalls putting in long, 20 hour days of study and effort, accruing the necessary knowledge and skills and gaining all the accreditations that would set his resume apart. In the end, his efforts paid off and he did in fact secure the position that he had sought, defying all the odds and bolstering his own long-held belief in the value of hard work and determination.

However, Steven was no stranger to the idea. Since a very young age, he had been putting in long hours running a large landscape business and saving up money to realize his ambitions. Further, while still in high school Steven would wake up well before he had to be at school and snow plow driveways in the neighborhood for money. From there he would take off to his classes, only to return to the snow plow truck for more work during his lunch break. Each day was a grueling schedule of taxing physical labor and demanding schoolwork, but Steven managed to pull through because he knew that the goal he was ultimately working towards would be worth it. The work ethic that he had to muster up in order to adhere to this strict regimen, which afforded him little to no free time, was frequently described by others as "unreal". As Steven himself says: **"My religion was work."** Twenty-four seven, from sun-up to sun-down, Steven worked, all with an end goal in mind.

He went on to play hockey in college, but before that could take him very far, he suffered an injury that forced him off the ice for quite a while. During his downtime, he was forced to look around himself and draw stark comparisons about his likelihood to succeed when measured against that of those around him. Finding himself not coming up as far ahead of the pack as he would have liked, Steven realized it was time to take a different approach, one that would get him into an office job where his determination would never be impeded by matters of physical happenstance.

In line with this new ambition, he obtained an internship at Business Methods, which eventually led to Chase. After securing the job with Chase Manhattan Bank as a result of his tireless labor, his end goal seemed all the more attainable.

Steven worked with Chase and Fleet Bank as a commercial banker for years, eventually achieving the title of 2nd Vice President before he returned to Business Methods at the age of 29 to work for them as their company president. From the moment he signed on with them, he says, he knew that he would one day buy the company. His first job, however, was pulling the business out of the brink of bankruptcy.

After running BMI for 7 years, he bought the company. Having achieved success by pulling BMI from the brink of financial disaster and finally acquiring the company, he then proceeded to grow it, adding value. His hard work and persistence finally paid off and he sold BMI to Toshiba in 2004.

Steven stayed on as president of Toshiba Business Solutions New York, the company that Business Methods eventually sold to, and he couldn't be happier. He is living out his dream, owing it all to the hard work and effort he invested while he was young. Moreover, he accredits much of his success to the two turning points of his life: being injured while playing hockey, which forced him to more accurately analyze his position in life, and the rigors of the training he had to undergo to make himself competitive for the job at Chase.

Over the years, Steven Sauer has learned quite a lot about what it takes to succeed in the world of business, and he is eager to help out young people similar to himself who have their own dreams of working for themselves and on their own terms.

Convinced that **beyond hard work and perseverance, networking is the most important skill that a young businessperson can learn**, Steve frequently delivers lectures to college kids on this very topic.

He says that **leveraging with the right person can spell all the difference**.

For that reason he advises that they go out while they're still young and become actively involved in the community as he did, taking advantage of the many opportunities to network with professionals that are bound to pay off later in life when they're looking for their all-too-crucial first jobs.

More than most people, Steven is qualified to expound upon the importance of such matters and what it takes to get exactly where you want to go in life. That he, being such an astonishing success in his own right, is willing to impart his knowledge to the rest of us is a benevolent gesture that speaks volumes about his love for business, the content of his character, and especially his ongoing commitment to the traditional values that won him his own success: hard work, determination, and a willingness to do what it takes to get the job done.

Turning Points

Phil Saunders

Chairman of Griffith Energy and Genesee Regional Bank

"How you spend your time is more important than how you spend your money. Money mistakes can be corrected, but time is gone forever."
David Norris

The story of Phil Saunders' life is one of constantly overcoming obstacles. As such, it only makes sense that his turning point would be the time when he was faced with one of the biggest obstacles that can be thrown against a person. Nevertheless, Phil has always had strength of character, and with each challenge he manages to overcome, he's only grown stronger. Before we can describe the turning point that changed Phil's life and put him firmly on the path to success, however, we need a bit of background information.

Phil's early home life was anything but what one would call happy. Phil's father was always something of a frightful influence in his life, but at the age of 13, Phil realized the true gravity of the situation. His father was a heavy drinker and on

top of that he frequently abused Phil's mother. The situation came to something of a head for Phil when during that same year, while his mother was driving him and his brother to a basketball practice, she suddenly steered the car into a ditch for seemingly no reason. Phil realized that his mother was driving while intoxicated, and from then on his family situation was beyond dire. He shouldered the responsibility of raising his sister and quickly became very independent in regards to taking care of himself. Moreover, the basketball practice that his mother had been driving him and his brother to was something of a horror in and of itself. Phil had achieved a great deal of success in sports, and rather than pride, his father felt only rage and jealousy towards him because of this. Realizing that the time was rapidly approaching when he would need to fend for himself, Phil made a resolution. His turning point had come.

"I started thinking about how to make myself financially viable. My first little project was to make water skis."

This "little project" shaped up to be Phil's first taste of running his own business, and he proved to have quite a knack for it. First of all, and completely on his own, he identified the importance of having a niche in the marketplace. Because he was an avid water skier, but had never been able to find skis that met his standards, he decided to start there. He took a guided tour of a water ski factory in order to take a look at how they did things, identified the areas where he thought they had gone wrong, and then decided how to improve upon it himself. He went home that very day and got started manufacturing his own water skis, an undertaking that would last him throughout high school.

While he was in high school, Phil's predictions proved correct, and his life under his father's roof came to a sudden end. During Phil's senior year, he impregnated his girlfriend, and his father demanded that he be allowed to pay for the girl to travel to Canada and receive an abortion. Phil absolutely refused, saying that the two of them preferred to have the child. Enraged, his father, who was President of the school board, got him kicked out of school and told him to leave home. Without even a completed high school education, Phil was on his own.

Luckily for him, he had already learned about the importance of finding a niche and excelling in it. Phil moved into a six room hotel with a shared bathroom and married his girlfriend. He continued to work his way into college, where he resumed playing baseball, paving his own way in an area where he had exceptional talent. Somewhat unexpectedly, Phil's father returned around this time and began to talk to him again. Now that he didn't have to live under his roof, Phil found his relationship with the man somewhat more palatable and he agreed to go to work at the truck stop that his father was partial owner of. Before long, he was presented with the opportunity to purchase a full third of the business for himself; using his savings, he seized upon the opportunity.

During his time working at this truck stop, Phil's knack for picking up on unfilled niches would pay off big time. During slow hours, he would often listen in and even carry on his own conversations with the truck drivers who had stopped in for a bite to eat. Over time, he realized that there was a common trend among what they had to say. The general consensus was that there was a lonely stretch of highway through the state of Virginia, where a truck stop was sorely needed. The oil companies in the area only considered it financially viable to build standard gas stations, and so full service truck stops were nowhere to be seen.

Phil recognized the opportunity for what it was and right away, he set out to find an oil company who was willing to listen to his idea and assist him with building a full service truck stop along that stretch of highway. He found someone and secured the financing, building his stop right next to the interstate where business promised to be good.

And good it was. During the years between ages 18 and 35, Phil did enough business at his truck stop to go on to sell the business, and as a result had enough money to retire in total comfort. However, so far he has chosen not to. For him, he said the aim was never to retire and do nothing, it was simply to:

> "...**approach the challenge that business offers and find the weak point, the niche that needed to be filled in order to solve the puzzle and succeed in the best way possible**."

It is exactly this tendency for overcoming obstacles that has gotten Phil to the level of success that he enjoys today. His life still continues to see its fair share of hardship, of course. In 1971 his father died of prostate cancer just when Phil's relationship with him had finally begun to take a turn for the better. By then, his father had already been divorced from Phil's mother, who had taken her own life in 1968. However, it is these very challenges early on that helped Phil develop the strength of character to recognize and go after opportunities full force when they presented themselves. This perseverance in the face of some of the darkest tragedies is what separates Phil from others who have given up along the way; in every sense of the word, it has made all the difference.

Peter Schottland

President and CEO of American Packaging Corporation

"All who have accomplished great things have had a great aim, have fixed their gaze on a goal which was high, one which sometimes seemed impossible."
Orison Swett Marden

If Peter Schottland's success is easily distilled to a single core attribute of his, it would with certainty be his ability to turn a bad situation around to work in his favor. Beginning with his earliest days, it could be said that Peter had more than his share of challenges. It was his ability to overcome difficulty that has determined the outcome in each situation and he considers each one of these challenges a turning point on his road to success. As we'll see, with each one of them, Peter has become a stronger person.

To begin with, when Peter was six years old, his mother became ill and was hospitalized for months. Peter was not allowed to see her and it was a stressful time for a little boy. Soon afterwards he was diagnosed with psoriasis. In order

149

to treat this, he had to wear cumbersome plastic gloves and make near constant use of a medicinal cream called Salva. As anyone with public school experience could probably guess, Peter was the victim of endless harassment by his peers.

During his sixth and seventh grade years, he was actually transferred between schools no less than four times in an attempt to find a better learning environment for him. In his seventh grade year he was sent to a private school, but then asked to leave due to poor performance after only seven weeks. As the youngest of three siblings, with a father who was constantly working, Peter found that he had little choice but to "figure things out for himself".

Despite these difficulties, Peter said that he learned three critical things from the experience. Firstly, he became fiercely independent. Secondly, he developed the ability to quickly make friends, something that would prove invaluable at his first job some years later. Lastly, and perhaps most importantly, he developed a thick skin and the ability to persevere. As he himself puts it: **"Taking rejection became my specialty."**

Although he finished high school ranked near the bottom of his class (195 out of 220), he defied the projections made about him, fought his way into college and graduated with a degree in business. Peter came to realize something from his time in college, which was that although he hadn't begun from the best set of circumstances, there was nothing inhibiting him from setting and meeting realistic goals. In short, there was nothing to hold him back from success. As he puts it:

"I came home after my freshman year in college thinking I had done well with a 2.3 GPA, but in reality I had greatly disappointed my father. I made a decision that I was going to get a 3.5 GPA, because I wanted to and found that if I set my

***mind to it, then I would achieve the goal. This
taught me I can do anything I want if I put my
mind to it."***

Shortly thereafter, he secured his first job as a salesman
with a Wall Street firm known as Kidder-Peabody. He recalls
feeling that it was something of a dream job, as they sent
him to Manhattan to train him, during which time he
experienced a very glitzy and luxurious lifestyle. What he
wasn't quite prepared for was the actual nature of the job,
which consisted of making several hundred cold calls a day in
an effort to generate sales. At first, Peter had a difficult time
of this and even wondered if his hard-won job was in
jeopardy, when he experienced a breakthrough that changed
his entire way of thinking; that qualifies as the second of his
major turning points.

During a call to a potential client, he recognized the person
as one of his neighbors and said so. As soon as he brought
that up, he noticed that the person became much more
receptive to his calling and he was able to get his pitch
across much more clearly. His sales took an upturn and Peter
caught on to a new tactic. Drawing on his schoolyard ability
to quickly make friends, he introduced himself to nearly
everyone as "someone who lives in the area", or "a
neighbor", and was genuinely amazed at the change in
attitude it inspired in people. Within no time at all, he was
one of the top sellers in the firm, and it was a joke around
the office that Peter lived within 1 to 2 miles of every person
in the Philadelphia area.

At the age of 29, however, Peter left his successful position
at the firm for an opportunity to join the family business.
The company, American Packaging Corp., had an office in
Rochester and before long Peter found himself shipped off
there from Philadelphia. He was to run the plant, which at
first was an exciting prospect, but he quickly realized that
there is more to a deal than meets the eye. The
previous management had serious quality and productivity
issues. The plant was staffed heavily with ex-convicts, and a

severe drug and alcohol problem existed. As Peter puts it, it was "like walking into the wild, wild West".

Nevertheless, Peter was used to dealing with difficult situations and devoted himself to turning the situation around. Despite considerable stumbling blocks, including threats on his and his family's lives and explosive demolition of their mailbox, Peter eventually succeeded in his vision, and his Rochester plant became one of the most successful in the whole company.

Between 1996 and 1999, the family business began to fall on hard times. Because of his successful track record at the Rochester plant, Peter was elected as the company's CEO in December 1999. At first, he was quite pleased with the outcome, but like most things in Peter's life, he was soon faced with difficulty and incredible obstacles. No more than two weeks after his appointment and promotion, the bank that had financed the business pulled their loan. Peter was faced with the prospect of finding the money to pay them off and the massive task of keeping the business afloat in the process.

This being one of his greatest challenges, Peter felt the pressure of the entire family counting on him for survival until his wife Susan, with a few subtle words, reminded him that he had already faced and overcome worse obstacles than this. "What's the worst that could happen?" she asked him. Peter said, "We can sell all the operations, except for Wisconsin, and survive." Susan's response was "No problem. Just let me know when you want to look for homes, and we'll sell everything here and move." **What Susan had done was to remove the fear of failure and taken much of the pressure off of Peter's shoulders.** For the first time, Peter took an objective look at his circumstances, and not surprisingly, found a way out. In the end, he did pay off the loan and turn the business around.

Without a doubt, Peter has faced significant difficulties throughout all areas of his life, both personal and professional. Nevertheless, thanks to the lessons he learned and took to heart as a child, he has always faced them with courage and conviction and found ways to overcome them. Bolstered by his turning points, to this day, Peter continues to challenge himself and expand his horizons with business ventures, confident that no matter what challenges arise, he will prove to be more than a match for them.

Turning Points

<u>Lori Van Dusen</u>

Managing Director Citi Smith Barney

"Pain is temporary, quitting is forever."
Lance Armstrong

Lori Van Dusen's turning points are many, and they are best described in her own words:

"There were many circumstances in my life that presented obstacles, but I tried to turn them all into positives."

Lori had a family life that she describes as being a very happy one, but in retrospect it is quite easy to see how in some ways it did estrange her from the common mindset of the time in which she grew up. But while others would have been alienated by these differences and dwelled upon them, Lori indeed turned them into strengths and capitalized upon them to become one of the pioneers in her field of investment.

To start at the beginning, Lori's first major source of inspiration was her grandfather. He was a successful man, despite having only an 8th grade education, and had a love for the stock market. In addition, he was a strong mentor and role model, and as a result Lori grew up without distinguishing very much at all between genders. For her, there were no distinctions between careers for men and careers for women. This enlightened viewpoint, however, wasn't one shared by many other people at the time.

Lori's ambition throughout the entirety of her childhood had been to be a singer. She had always dreamed of performing on Broadway and had been recognized for many years as a talented singer. When the time came for her to graduate high school, she prepared to apply to various music schools around the country. However, her vocal teacher stepped in at that point in time and asked her if she might want to reconsider. Lori did have quite a bit of talent, but as a soprano, the field was competitive. In other words, as her teacher put it, voices like hers were "a dime a dozen".

Lori was devastated. She had been told by someone that she highly respected that she simply wasn't good enough. But instead of dwelling on the negative aspects of this circumstance, Lori decided to take her teacher's criticism seriously and professionally, rather than personally. She applied to go to a liberal arts college where she could sample other disciplines and learn what else she liked before making up her mind about what career to embark upon.

It was upon first arriving at college that she experienced what can only be called culture shock. Lori realized that her family and the lifestyle she grew up in were far from the norm. Whereas Lori's grandfather had given her a sense of valuing the person without considering their gender or background, many others felt differently. Moreover, Lori had grown up with three parents. Her mother was divorced. This was embraced as normal within her extended family. But, Lori soon realized that coming from a "broken home" had a stigma attached to it. In spite of this difference that could have driven a wedge between her and others, Lori realized this made her unique. It was a difficult experience to be sure, but it only made her stronger and more persistent.

Her attitude was always a good one and she made a lot of friends. The continuation of her habit of turning negatives into positives would set her up for the next major stage in her life.

While getting her education, Lori realized that what she liked most of all was simply being around other people, talking to them, finding out what they liked and carrying on conversations. Appropriately, she decided that a position in business where she could capitalize on her people skills would be great for her and she resolved to become either a College President or to run a company. Eventually, Lori decided to follow in her grandfather's footsteps and enter the financial services field.

On her first day of work in the industry, she learned that she was the only financial advisor who was a woman in the entire office, as well as the youngest financial advisor. She worked hard to overcome the obstacles that were placed in front of her and to be taken seriously by the others. At times, it seemed as if the more successful she became, the more obstacles there were. Lori was meeting and exceeding objectives more rapidly than anyone had expected, and besides that she was doing some very pioneering work in her industry. All of this spawned quite a bit of jealousy.

Drawing upon her main strength of turning negatives into positives, Lori simply redoubled her efforts and used the jealousy and negative attention to "fuel the fire" of her ambitions. She continued to focus and began to establish clear goals within the field and meet them despite a very difficult work environment. Lori eventually became known within the industry for her pioneering wealth management model. The success stemming from that breakthrough has carried forward ever since, and today Lori is recognized as one of the top financial advisors in the nation.

When asked about the secrets to her success, Lori reflects on the numerous marathons that she has run. There are points in the race when she wanted to rip the tag off her jersey and quit. Runners call it "hitting the wall". For Lori, it's exhilarating and most rewarding when her mind overcomes the obstacle of pain, as she moves forward to complete the race. She relates this to the long journey that life and her business both present. Lori comments that her uncommon background has helped her to avoid the typical pitfalls that she's seen so many of her co-workers fall into. Rather than fall down in front of an obstacle, Lori simply thinks about what will work and what won't, and approaches things from a quirky angle that is right in line with her upbringing. To put things simply, she is successful because she is consistent, she never gives up, and she's willing to put in the hard work necessary to turn unfavorable situations into favorable ones.

<u>Tom Wilmot</u>

Chairman of the Board Wilmorite Corporation

"You will never achieve big results in your life without consistent and persistent action."
Les Hewitt

Tom Wilmot's journey to the top began at a very young age when he first grasped the values of independent thinking. Today he's known for being a mall developer, and with buildings all over the east coast, this is certain to be his long-standing legacy. However, this didn't spring up overnight. It never would have happened had Tom not prepared the fertile soil of independent thought and risk-taking that would allow his ideas to one day bear fruit. The story of his success goes hand in hand with his philosophical development.

From a very young age, Tom was no stranger to hard work. His father had many business interests, but was primarily in the real estate and construction business. Further, the family grew up

159

on a farm and his father was a strict disciplinarian. When he gave an order, it was to be interpreted as law. While Tom certainly respected his father and the power of the businesses that he had built up, he credits this authoritarian approach to parenting with instilling the need for independent thinking in him. Ironically, it is that same deep-seated thinking that would one day expand the family business beyond its boundaries and into the multi-million dollar enterprise that it is today.

In addition to his psychological development as a far-reaching thinker in response to his father's strictness, Tom was also introduced to the value of a strong work ethic. Living on a farm, he always had plenty of chores to do after school, and they would often keep him busy until the sun went down. In order to give himself a temporary reprieve from this labor, Tom sought out an escape in the form of... more work. He took a part time job in construction, which would prove to be the second cornerstone in shaping his unique career.

While working in construction, Tom marveled at how each job required a huge number of skilled specialists. From the laborers to the masons, Tom worked alongside each of them and learned their trade. By the time he had been on the construction job several months, he found himself enamored with the tangible, finished buildings that construction work offered as a testament to a job well done. Though he had always planned to go to work for the family business, Tom knew then and there that he wanted to be intimately involved in construction.

He entered Syracuse University in 1966, where he got his degree in Civil Engineering. His first plan was to be an architect and to do the actual design work on buildings. He quickly realized that he lacked the technical drawing ability to keep up with the others in the class - and this was well before the days of computer assisted design programs. Not willing to totally forsake his dream to be involved in construction, Tom decided to go into the more theoretical side of things and that's how he came to get his degree in Civil Engineering.

The very day after he graduated from Syracuse in 1970, Tom went back to the family business in order to go to work. Though it wasn't quite what he imagined, he felt the desire to help out where he was needed and began working in the field. It was only a short matter of time before he was promoted to the position of an assistant estimator and began to take on more and more responsibility.

In 1978, Tom's uncle, who was intimately involved with work in the family business, had a heart attack. Tom was suddenly left with a lot more responsibility than he had ever handled before. He was only 27 years old at the time, but was now expected to perform the duties that had previously been handled by his uncle – responsibilities on the level of a senior vice president.

Just two short years later, Tom's own father would die of cancer and Tom's responsibility to the family business would find itself redoubled once more. It being the late 1970's, the economy was falling on bad times as well making matters especially difficult for Tom.

However, being no stranger to independent thinking thanks to his upbringing, and being equally familiar with risk-taking and hard work, Tom decided to totally redefine the family business that he was now head of. He imagined the business as a small development firm, a place where he could flex his civil engineering muscle on construction projects such as mall development. The bad economy put a damper on things with interest rates in the neighborhood of 18-20%, but Tom nevertheless persevered.

Tom bought the Danbury Connecticut Fairgrounds for a sum of 25 million dollars. Considering the terrible state of the economy at that time and the high interest on his loans, this meant an incredibly high degree of risk for Tom. If he hadn't managed to make a success out of this investment, he stood to lose literally everything he had.

As Tom puts it, he hardly even thought of it as radical, risk-taking behavior at the time; it was just what he wanted to do.

> **"When you're young, you don't necessarily see the risks, you just take them. It's a roll of the dice... a gamble..."**

Tom developed his first mall on that land and met with a great deal of success. Since then, he has gradually built his business up, buying larger and larger plots of land, and designing and planning more and more intricate shopping mall projects. Today, he is known as a successful mall developer.

Nowadays, Tom has four grown children. Three of them have joined him in the family business, with one still in school. Although they work for the company, it should come as no surprise that their father has instilled them all with a sense of the importance of autonomous thinking. **Even within the context of the family business, they always strive to make their own individual mark and to leave behind their own unique impression on whatever deals they are a part of.** Having imparted the values that led to his own unparalleled success to his children, it seems certain to say that Tom's success will continue to live on for many generations to come, as a testament to the power of individualistic thought and solid work ethic.

Louise Woerner

Chairman and CEO of Home Care of Rochester

"I am in the world to change the world."
Käthe Kollwitz

The turning points of Louise Woerner's life all seem intertwined, in a sense. Almost predestined, they would one day coalesce into a skilful balance between the two extremes that Louise was always forced to occupy: the aggressive feminist fighting for recognition against the prejudice of her time, and the caring woman who merely wanted to succeed on her own terms. With influences coming from her family life, her scholastic life, as well as her professional life, one might say that her whole life is a series of turning points, rather than one singular moment that made all the difference.

Nevertheless, let's start at the very beginning in order to understand the full scope of the story of Louise's success.

> ***One of her first and most important memories is sitting on the sill of a second floor window of her family's home where she played checkers with her maternal grandmother. One day, upon winning, she came to the sudden realization that her grandmother had let her win. She asked her why, only to receive the reply, "Because you love winning so much". This straightforward response opened Louise's eyes in a number of ways. First of all, it revealed to her the competitive aspect of her personality that could succeed in a career, even if the times were unfriendly to the idea of women working outside the home. Secondly, it instilled in her a world view wherein she felt gratitude for all the times others bestowed generosity upon her and helped her move ahead.***

Louise carried her "love of winning" over to school with her, where she achieved a high level of academic success, becoming what she describes as something of a "nerd". She recalls enjoying some aspects of the simplicity of that age, such as the fact that she and her family used to sit down to dinner every night together. It was at one such dinner that she had another eye opening experience.

Her father asked her what exactly she planned to major in while in school. When Louise replied that she wished to become a lawyer like her father, he casually responded with the off-hand assertion that there had never been a good woman lawyer, and that there was no reason she should think that she would be the first.

Such a comment was reflective of the times that Louise grew up in. However, she did retain an encouraging influence in the form of her mother, a visionary who saw that women would have more choices in the future. She encouraged Louise to pursue anything she wanted to, even while her father was urging her to take sewing classes and other traditionally feminine subjects.

When Louise did go to college, she majored in business at Trinity University as an undergrad before going on to the University of Chicago to pursue her MBA degree. She was able to attend Trinity on a full scholarship as a result of her academic prowess. Actually, her first scholarship was to Stanford, but she was unable to accept that offer because of her family's reluctance to send her all the way across the country to California.

While at Trinity, she worked all throughout school as the secretary to the chairman of the department, Ray Erlandson. This offered quite a lot of good experience in more ways than one. For starters, she learned much about business from her close contact with the faculty, and internalizing their credo that **management is about "getting things done through people"**. However, she also learned that expectations for women would extend beyond the walls of her own home, when Erlandson told her that he would disown any daughter of his who left Trinity without being married. In addition, she saw that she was the only female in her classes, so she knew that there was going to be a tough fight ahead of her. It occurred to her for the first time that the advice of people like her father and Erlandson wasn't intended to be cruel, but rather just reflected the reality of the times: it was going to be incredibly difficult for a woman to succeed in business, and they simply wanted to protect her. Nevertheless Louise remained determined to succeed.

After graduating from the University of Chicago, she met yet another mentor figure, Joe Halbach. It was here that she experienced another of her turning points when Halbach offered what he said was critical advice: that she had to get the feminist chip off her shoulder in order to succeed. Louise realized that it was in fact limiting to view things through the perspective of herself against the world, and she began to try to see things as a more level battlefield, even if that wasn't entirely the case.

The change resulting from that was fairly major, and Louise started to meet with more and more success. She was offered a job as an analyst in the Nixon White House by Halbach and accepted it. After the White House job, she went back into the private sector with a consulting firm. While there, she spent a lot of time doing research work on social security data. From this research, she began to realize certain trends, such as the growing age of the average worker, and the fact that she could easily capitalize upon this knowledge to fill a certain niche. Even in her own family, she realized that her father was completely unable to get along on his own after the death of her mother.

It occurred to Louise that she could turn the family values she had enjoyed as a child into a successful business, merging both aspects of her personality together into a cohesive whole. As a result she founded Home Care of Rochester, a service which offers the elderly home care assistance preparing meals and other domestic concerns. She met with a setback right off the bat when she had to contend with New York State regulations that forced her to re-brand her corporate identity as one that centered on health care in the home. She recalls all kinds of illuminating encounters, such as a luncheon with Max Farash, a real estate magnate of the Rochester community, who asked Louise what was the most money she had ever lost in a business deal. After she gave the answer, Farash said "well then you're tested". This helped her to realize what she calls her fundamental tenet of business:

"You have to be able to fail forward."

That realization to learn from failure, however, proved to be for the better. As one of the first home health care providers in the region, Louise went from three active employees to a full 640 full time employees in just a short amount of time.

Today, she spends most of her time working on a succession plan for her company, gradually passing ownership on to the employees so that the company and its reputation will survive her. When asked about the key to her success, Louise comments that for her, **money has always been about the ability to buy freedom of choice and freedom of time, rather than material possessions**. When she began to lose the desire to "prove herself" and focused on her desire to simply become successful on her own terms, bringing together all of her many influences into a single whole, she was able to move forward and grasp this simple truth that has since made all the difference.

Turning Points

<u>**Randy Schuster**</u>

<u>**About the Author**</u>

Randy Schuster is more than just a collector of inspiring stories about the turning points in the lives of successful people; he has lived such a story himself. The turning point in Randy's life occurred when he was 32 years old, sitting at a lonely desk with a phone in his hands, his eyes closed, and a very important vision flashing through his head. That moment would shape the course of his future - a future he had never really envisioned for himself but which seemed unavoidable. But to understand that moment we must know about how he arrived there.

When Randy was very young, he suffered from a learning disability that kept him out of regular classes. He came to the realization that simply by putting forth more effort he would be able to achieve the same level of accomplishment and perhaps even to go beyond it. As Randy puts it, this decision to simply bolster himself up and put forth the necessary effort to achieve his goals, no matter the obstacles in his way, is what has helped set him apart over the course of his personal and professional life.

Randy had a somewhat unique upbringing, but one that might seem somewhat familiar to those who have read the

169

rest of the success stories in this book. His family owned a business, Marjax Sporting Goods, which boasted over 20 stores in shopping malls throughout the Northeast. As such, he was exposed to the business environment from a very young age and saw the ins and outs of running a successful business firsthand. Perhaps it was this direct knowledge of how difficult it can be to succeed and stay ahead that drove him to overcome his own disabilities. Whatever the case, he knew from an early age what he wanted to do with his life. In the eighth grade, his school played host to a group of career counselors who came to speak to all the children about what they wanted to do with their futures. Randy wanted nothing more than to work in the family business that he had grown up in and to bring it to new heights of success.

With the goal established, he went on to become a finance major at Indiana University and eventually joined the family business in his late 20's. However, circumstances would convene that would threaten to derail the life he had envisioned for himself. At the age of 32, with two sons aged just 4 and 1, Randy was forced to watch as the family business closed down and his dreams were put on indefinite hold. It was more than just a time of disaster for Randy; it was also a time of reinvention. His family scattered across the country after the dissolution of Marjax and he was faced with innumerable opportunities as to where to go next. He contemplated moving south to Florida or west to California but eventually the decision he ultimately made, along with his wife Erni, was to stick it out in his home town of Rochester, NY because it seemed like the best place to raise their children.

Randy set about making a life for himself in Rochester and starting his own business in the financial services field. He started from the bottom up, sitting at a desk, making cold calls to total strangers. While he met his "3 appointments a day" goal on the first day, he quickly began to see this in a negative light: only 3 appointments out of eight hours in the office! This negative attitude began to overtake him and it came to a head on January 3rd, 1995, when he received a particularly nasty response to one of his telephone inquiries. As he hung up the phone, he vividly remembers just sitting at that desk with the receiver in his hands, and a vision came to him of his youngest son, then two years old, playing on the floor in an unfurnished living room. He recalled the efforts he had always put forth in life and that they had never yet failed him, and said to himself, "I have to do this, I have no choice; I must take care of my family and I really believe that what I do can help people and business owners." As he puts it: he opened his eyes and did it, as simple as that.

Immediately after that turning point, he went on to beat his previous day's goal of 3 appointments a day by gaining 5 appointments that afternoon alone. He has never looked back.

For over a decade, Randy has been one of the most successful financial advisors in the country. He's consistently ranked in the top 5% of his entire profession by the prestigious Million Dollar Round Table (MDRT), the premier association of financial professionals, and has been a guest speaker at numerous functions. He has carved out a unique niche within the industry by focusing on the coordination of planning, growing and protecting his clients' portfolio of assets. He guides his clients through the complex tax code, planning for business continuation and succession, transfer issues of privately held firms, and wealth accumulation strategies. He is the author of The Power of Habits-How to Be a Rainmaker, published in 2005 which sells out at the annual MDRT meetings.

Free eQuotes

This book was written to encourage young people to stay in Upstate New York. It is vitally important for the future of our community for our young people to see how successful they can be right here in our area. We hope that reading the stories of our fellow citizens helps young people to make the decision to stay here and build their careers in Rochester and the surrounding areas.

With that in mind, if you know any person who would be inspired by any of the stories, and would like a copy of some of the motivational quotes in these stories in an eQuote format please go to:

www.randyschuster.com

and click on the Free Turning Points eQuotes icon.

For more information on the author go to:

www.coordinatedplan.com

or call 585-899-1243.

For bulk purchases please call the above number.